Real Progress in
Writing

Steve Eddy and Kevin Dyke
Series Editor: Alan Howe

HODDER
EDUCATION
AN HACHETTE UK COMPANY

The publisher would like to thank the following for permission to reproduce copyright material:

Acknowledgements: p.7: Michelle Paver, from *Wolf Brother* (Orion, 2004)**; pp.11–14:** George Orwell, from *Animal Farm* (Martin Secker & Warburg, 1945), copyright © George Orwell 1945, reproduced by permission of Bill Hamilton as the Literary Executor of the Estate of the Late Sonia Brownell Orwell; **p.17:** Beverley Naidoo, from *The Other Side of Truth* (Penguin Books, 2000); **p.20:** Joan Didion, from *Slouching Towards Bethlehem* (Farrar, Straus & Giroux, 2008); **p.29:** J. B. Priestley, from *An Inspector Calls* (Penguin Books, 1969); **p.30:** Jon Mayhew, from *Mortlock* (Bloomsbury Publishing, 2010); **p.31:** Kim Edwards, from *The Memory Keeper's Daughter* (Penguin Books, 2007); **pp.32–34:** Lauren St John, from *Dead Man's Cove* (Orion Children's Books, 2010); **p.36–38:** David Yelland, from *The Truth about Leo* (Penguin Books, 2010), reproduced by permission of Penguin Books Ltd; **pp.40–41, 44:** J. K. Rowling, from *Harry Potter and the Goblet of Fire* (Bloomsbury Publishing, 2005), © J. K. Rowling 2000, reproduced by permission of The Blair Partnership; **p.71:** George Monbiot, 'As officials dither, fishing boats flout the law and rip out the life in our seas', from *The Guardian*, www.monbiot.com/2009/06/02/blue-desert (1 June, 2009), copyright Guardian News & Media Ltd 2009, reproduced by permission of the publisher; **p.73:** 'Starspot: Your daily horoscopes…decoded' (Taurus) from *Shout Magazine online* (April 21–May 21), reproduced by permission of DC Thomson; **pp.73:** Christy Brown, from *My Left Foot* (Martin Secker & Warburg, 1954); **p.75:** Bill Bryson, from *Notes from a Big Country* (Doubleday, 1998); 'Tobacco is a problem to be tackled, not dodged' from *Independent online* (2 May, 2013), www.independent.co.uk, reproduced by permission of ESI Media; **p.77:** Jan Moir, 'I can't take any more of these sad, deluded wannabes' from *Mail online* (3 May, 2013), reproduced by permission of Solo Syndication; **p.79:** Dea Birkett, 'Cruel? No, elephants love the circus' from *Daily Mail* (25 February, 2009), reproduced by permission of Solo Syndication; Benjamin Zephaniah, 'Animals in circuses: a modern-day slave trade' from *The Guardian* (30 November, 2012), copyright Guardian News & Media Ltd 2012, reproduced by permission of the publisher; **p.81:** Speeches by Barack Obama, Hillary Clinton, and Martin Luther King; **p.83:** Ted Hughes, from *The Iron Man* (Faber & Faber, 1968); **p.85:** George Orwell, from *Down and Out in Paris and London* (Victor Gollancz, 1933); **p.89:** Melvin Burgess, from *The Baby and Fly Pie* (Andersen Press, 1993); **p.91:** Andy Milligan, from *Riddlestrop* (Simon & Schuster UK, 2009); **p.101:** Kathleen McMahon, from *Social Media Scams*, copyright © 2013 Kathleen McMahon; **p.103:** 'The Earth's climate is changing, and people's activities are the main cause' from www.epa.gov/climatestudents/basics/index.html; **p.105:** 'Turkey', from Rough Guides website, www.roughguides.com/destinations/europe/turkey/where-to-go, reproduced by permission of Penguin Books Ltd; **p.107:** Emma Levine, from *A Game of Polo with a Headless Goat* (Andre Deutsch, 2000); **p.113:** 'Beach safety advice' from http://rnli.org/safetyandeducation/stayingsafe/beach-safety/Pages/Beach-safety-advice.aspx, reproduced by permission of the Royal National Lifeboat Institution; **p.117:** Patrick Bateson, Zoological Society of London, 'Do we need zoos?'; **p.121:** Stephen Harris, 'Do we need zoos?' from *The Times*, reproduced by permission of the author; **p.125:** Ian Thomson, 'My Hero: Usain Bolt' from *The Guardian* (27 July, 2012), copyright Guardian News & Media Ltd 2012, reproduced by permission of the publisher; **p.127:** Ellen MacArthur, from *Taking on the World* (Michael Joseph, 2002), reproduced by permission of Penguin Books Ltd; **p.129:** Kari Herbert, from *The Explorer's Daughter* (Penguin Books, 2006); **p.131:** Martin Douglas Mitchinson, 'A Dugout Canoe in the Darien Gap' from *The Darien Gap: Travels in the Rainforest of Panama* (Harbour Publishing, 2008), copyright © 2008 by Martin Douglas Mitchinson, reproduced by permission of the publisher; **p.133, 155:** Gerald Durrell, from *My Family and Other Animals* (Rupert Hart-Davis, 1956); **pp.134–35:** Andrew Matthews, from *Excuses, Excuses*; Rosa Guy, 'She' in *Sixteen Stories: Short Stories by Outstanding Writers for Young Adults*, edited by Douglas Gallo (Bantam Doubleday Dell Books for Young Readers, 1984), © 1984 by Rosa Guy; Sydney J. Bounds, from 'The Ghost Train' in *The Kingfisher Treasury of Spooky Stories*. Chosen by Jane Olliver (Kingfisher Books, 2004) © Sydney J. Bounds, 1972; **p.136:** Barack Obama, Speech, 25 June 2013; **p.139:** Barry Hines and Allan Stronach, from *Kes – A Play of the Novel* (Heinemann London, 1983); **p.141:** Mark Taylor, 'Rescuers pull 58 charity swimmers from the sea', www.theguardian.com/uk/2013/may/26/charity-swimmers-rescued-sea; **p.143:** Richard Branson, from *Losing My Virginity* (Virgin Books, 2007); **p.145:** 'Running to music' from www.nhs.uk/Livewell/c25k/Pages/running-music.aspx, © Crown copyright; **p.147:** 'Liverpool' from Rough Guides website, www.roughguides.com/destinations/europe/england/north-west/liverpool, reproduced by permission of Penguin Books Ltd; **p.151:** 'One tycoon, a whale massacre and dog food', petition appeal from Avaaz.org; **p.153:** Nick Evans, 'Experience: I saved a baby who fell from a window' from *The Guardian* (19 January, 2013), copyright Guardian News & Media Ltd 2013, reproduced by permission of the publisher; **p.157:** Mary Hoffman, from *Chicken*; Beverley Naidoo, from *Poinsettias* in *Global Tales: Stories from Many Cultures* (Longman, 1997); **p.159:** Kathleen Jamie, from 'Sightlines' (Sort Of Books, 2012).

Permission for re-use of © Crown copyright information is granted under the terms of the Open Government Licence (OGL).

Every effort has been made to trace and contact copyright holders. The publishers will be glad to rectify any errors or omissions at the earliest opportunity.

Photo credits: p.4: © Getty Images/iStockphoto/Thinkstock; **p.6:** © Back Page Images/Rex Features; **p.9:** © hotshotsworldwide/Fotolia; **p.11:** © E. Spek/Fotolia; **p.13:** © kohy/Fotolia; **p.14:** © moorhen/Getty Images/iStockphoto/Thinkstock; **p.15:** © erniboesen/Fotolia; **p.16:** ©Balint Radu/Fotolia; **p.18:** © dpa picture alliance archive/Alamy; **p.20:** © Wirepec/Fotolia; **pp.21, 25:** Image created by Reto Stöckli, Nazmi El Saleous, and Marit Jentoft-Nilsen, NASA GSFC; **p.23:** © James Steidl/ Fotolia; **p.24:** © Natalia Lukiyanova/Getty Images/iStockphoto/Thinkstock; **p.25:** © Image created by Reto Stöckli, Nazmi El Saleous, and Marit Jentoft-Nilsen, NASA GSFC **(top)**, Photodisc/Getty Images **(bottom)**; **p.29:** © theatrepix/Alamy; **p.31:** © Performance Image/Alamy; **p.34:** © Galyna Andrushko/Fotolia; **p.35:** © DEAD MAN'S COVE by Lauren St John, illustrated by David Dean, published by Orion Children's Books; **p.38:** © Ned White/Getty Images/iStockphoto/ Thinkstock; **p.39:** © London News Pictures/Rex Features; **p.45:** © industrieblick/Fotolia; **p.46:** © Neil Hall/Reuters/Corbis; **p.48:** © Ingus Evertovskis/Fotolia; **p.53:** © Getty Images/Ingram Publishing/Thinkstock; **p.54:** © Sergey Belov /Fotolia; **p.57:** © dedMazay/Fotolia; **p.58:** © Jasmin Merdan/Fotolia; **p.61:** © michaeljung/Fotolia; **p.62:** © Thomas Northcut/Photodisc/Getty/Thinkstock; **p.64:** © Vasiliy Koval/Fotolia; **p.66:** © Photodisc/Getty/Thinkstock; **p.71:** © Duncan Noakes/Fotolia; **p.75:** © nito/Fotolia; **p.78:** © Andrea Izzotti/Fotolia; **p.81:** © Rex Features **(top)**; © Zhang Jun/Xinhua Press/Corbis **(centre)**, © Everett Collection/Rex Features **(bottom)**; **p.83:** © karaboux/Fotolia; **p.85:** © Luciano Mortula/Getty Images/iStockphoto/Thinkstock; **p.87:** © The Art Archive/Alamy; **p.89:** © CBH/Fotolia; **p.90:** © lassedesignen/ Fotolia; **p.93:** © Back Page Images/Rex Features; **p.94:** © Back Page Images/Rex Features; **p.97:** © micromonkey/Fotolia **(top)**, © CandyBox Images/Fotolia **(bottom)**; **p.101:** © Carsten Reisinger/Fotolia; **p.103:** © isidore/Fotolia; **p.105:** © Robert Harding World Imagery/Alamy; **p.107:** © Getty Images/iStockphoto/Thinkstock; **p.110:** © Jacek Chabraszewski/Fotolia; **p.111:** © Africa Studio/Fotolia; **p.113:** © Linda More/Fotolia; **p.115:** ©Anyka/Fotolia; **p.117:** © Tetyana/Fotolia; **p.121:** © Papirazzi/Fotolia; **p.123:** © Tetyana/Fotolia; **p.125:** © Yuri Kadobnov/AFP/Getty Images; **p.127:** © Rex Features; **p.129:** © Getty Images/iStockphoto/Thinkstock; **p.131:** © Henrik Larsson/ Fotolia; **p.133:** © charger_v8/Fotolia; **p.135:** © alexskopje/Fotolia; **p.136:** © Rex Features; **p.140:** © rdnzl/Fotolia; **p.141:** © Gail Johnson/Fotolia; **p.145:** © Andres Rodriguez/Fotolia; **p.151:** © Sebastian French/Fotolia; **p.155:** © brulove/Fotolia; **p.159:** © RKP/Fotolia.

Although every effort has been made to ensure that website addresses are correct at time of going to press, Hodder Education cannot be held responsible for the content of any website mentioned. It is sometimes possible to find a relocated web page by typing in the address of the home page for a website in the URL window of your browser.

Orders: please contact Bookpoint Ltd, 130 Milton Park, Abingdon, Oxon OX14 4SB. Telephone: (44) 01235 827720. Fax: (44) 01235 400454. Lines are open 9.00–17.00, Monday to Saturday, with a 24-hour message answering service. Visit our website at www.hoddereducation.co.uk

© Steve Eddy, Kevin Dyke 2014
First published in 2014 by
Hodder Education
An Hachette UK Company,
Carmelite House, 50 Victoria Embankment
London EC4Y 0DZ

Impression number   5 4 3
Year   2018

Typeset in ITC Garamond Std Light by Aptara, Inc.

Printed in Dubai

A catalogue record for this title is available from the British Library

ISBN 978 1 444 16898 3

Contents

Know how to control and vary sentence types for effect on your reader

1

Know how to choose sentence types for different purposes

I am learning to use a variety of sentence types to:

→ make my writing interesting for the reader

→ choose sentence types for particular purposes

→ combine sentence types for different effects.

Activity 1 | Identify and write simple sentences

Sentences can have different functions:

- question
- statement
- command
- exclamation.

1 Identify the functions of these simple sentences.

The lion roars. Will it attack? Run! Aaaagh!

2 Write your own sentences like the ones above, including all four functions.

Activity 2 | Write statement sentences

The most common sentence type is a **statement**, giving you a complete piece of information. A short statement sentence may include just a subject and a verb, like this:

Mandy (subject) drove (verb).

A statement sentence can also have an object:

Mandy drove **the car**.

A statement sentence can also include adverbs and adjectives:

Mandy drove the **new** (adjective) car **carefully** (adverb).

1 Write two statement sentences, choosing some of the following words.

man	tiger	girl		window-cleaner	ball
ladder	the	devoured	climbed		kicks

2 Rewrite your two sentences, or make up new ones using the words listed. Add at least one adjective or adverb to each sentence to add some extra detail.

Activity 3 | Divide up sentences correctly

Even a very short statement sentence should begin with a capital letter and end with a full stop. It is not enough to add a comma, like this:

Carina sneezed, she had a cold.

This should be:

Carina sneezed. She had a cold.

1 Rewrite these two sentences using correct punctuation.

a) The lake dried up, it had been a long hot summer.

b) Puffins are sea birds, they live on fish.

2 Rewrite this student paragraph with correct punctuation.

I walked to the edge of the dried-up lake, in the middle I could see something sticking up out of the mud, from here it looked like a sword, I wondered if it was old, and perhaps valuable, I was worried that I'd get stuck in the mud trying to reach it, which could be dangerous, despite this, I took off my shoes and socks, rolled up my jeans, and stepped onto the baked mud, it cracked a little, like Easter egg chocolate.

Activity 4 | Turn phrases into sentences

A phrase is a group of words that do not in themselves make a sentence. For example, 'The bright red car' would need a verb to be a sentence:

The bright red car **crashed**.

This is a complete sentence because the verb now tells us something about the subject (the bright red car). You can also add further details:

The bright red car crashed through the plate-glass window.

This is still a sentence, because it is made up of a subject and predicate.

1 Add some more words to make each phrase a complete sentence.

a) African elephants

b) Skateboarders in the car park

c) Failure to pay attention

> **Key terms**
> A clause has two main parts:
> **Subject:** occurs with (and often before) a verb; is usually a noun or a noun phrase
> **Predicate:** the part of the clause that follows the subject. Typically it is made up of a verb and what follows the verb.

Activity 5 | Join sentences using conjunctions

You can join two or more sentences together using **conjunctions**. The commonest conjunction is **and**:

The brakes squealed **and** the lorry came to a halt.

In this example, two main clauses are linked together. This is called co-ordination. Other conjunctions show how the sentence parts relate to each other. The commonest of these is **but**, showing a contrast:

I like cheese **but** I hate olives.

> **Key terms**
> **Conjunctions:** words that link words or clauses within a sentence (e.g. 'but')
> **Connectives:** words or phrases that link clauses or sentences (e.g. 'On the other hand')

1 Turn the following single-clause sentences into multi-clause sentences, using conjunctions from this list.

and	but	so
then	or	yet

a) Last night I went to the cinema. I caught the bus home.

b) It started to rain. She put up the umbrella.

c) I tried the doorbell. Nobody answered.

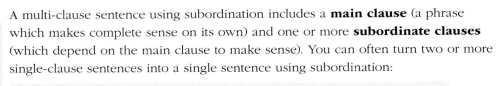

Activity 6   Turn single-clause sentences into multi-clause sentences using subordination

A multi-clause sentence using subordination includes a **main clause** (a phrase which makes complete sense on its own) and one or more **subordinate clauses** (which depend on the main clause to make sense). You can often turn two or more single-clause sentences into a single sentence using subordination:

Scrooge was a tight-fisted old man. He hated Christmas. (Single-clause)

Scrooge, who was a tight-fisted old man, hated Christmas. (Subordinated)

You could add another subordinate clause:

Scrooge, who was a tight-fisted old man, hated Christmas, regarding it as a time when workers expected to be paid for doing nothing.

This has the advantage of combining all the important information about Scrooge into a single, complete sentence.

1 Combine the ideas in these single-clause sentences by using subordination.

a) Frank Lampard played for England. He began his career with West Ham.

b) Laura Robson was born in 1994. She won her first tennis tournament in 2008. This made her a star overnight.

2 Add new information to these sentences by using subordination.

a) The *Star Wars* films were hugely successful. (Use the **relative pronoun** 'which'.)

b) One Direction will appear in Manchester. (Use the **relative pronoun** 'who'.)

Key terms

Pronoun: word standing in place of a noun, like 'she' or 'it'

Relative pronoun: pronoun marking a relative clause, as in 'We saw Jo, **who** was ill.'

Activity 7   Vary where you put subordinate clauses

A subordinate clause can go before or after the main clause. If you want to emphasise one piece of information, you can do this by putting that clause first:

Although imprisoned for 27 years, Nelson Mandela became President of South Africa. (*Subordinate clause before main clause: emphasises the imprisonment*)

Jessica Ennis-Hill won a gold medal at the 2012 Olympics, which has made her a national hero. (*Subordinate clause after main clause: emphasises the achievement*)

1 Write a sentence about yourself, putting a subordinate clause **after** the main clause.

2 Write a sentence about someone you know, putting a subordinate clause **before** the main clause.

Activity 8 | Vary your use of sentences

1 Good writers vary their use of sentence types. They do this in order to create certain effects. Read the following passage and find at least one example of each main type of sentence: **single-clause**; **multi-clause** (coordination); **multi-clause** (subordination).

A stone-age boy is fighting an older boy in an enemy camp.

Torak tried his second trick. Feigning total incompetence, which wasn't hard, he hit out wildly, tempting Hord with a glimpse of his unprotected chest. Hord took the bait, but as his spear came in to strike, Torak's guard-arm swung across to meet it. Hord's spear-point sank into the thick hide guard, nearly knocking Torak off his feet, but Torak managed to keep to his plan by twisting his guard-arm sharply upwards. Hord's spear-shaft snapped in two. The watchers groaned. Hord staggered back without a spear.

Torak was astonished. He hadn't expected it to work.

Hord recovered swiftly. Lunging forwards, he jabbed his knife into Torak's spear-hand. Torak cried out as the flint bit between finger and thumb. He lost his footing and dropped his spear. Hord lunged again. Torak only just managed to roll away in time and scramble to his feet.

Now they were both spearless. Both down to knives. To gain some breathing space, Torak dodged behind the fire. His chest was heaving, and his wounded hand throbbed. Sweat was pouring down his sides. He bitterly regretted not copying Hord and taking off his jerkin.

Michelle Paver, *Wolf Brother*

---

2 Find where the author has used six single-clause sentences in a row (not all in the same paragraph). What effect do you think this has?
3 Find a sentence that uses subordination. Write it out and underline and label the main clause – the part of the sentence that makes complete sense on its own.
4 There is one sentence here that does not have a main verb – called a **minor** sentence. Can you find it? Explain why the writer might have decided to use it.

● ●

Activity 9 | Use a variety of sentence types in your own writing

1 Think of a possible argument that you could describe. Make some notes on:
   a) who is involved
   b) why they are arguing
   c) what they say and/or do to each other
   d) what happens.
2 Write your own account. Use a mixture of single and multi-clause sentences in a way that adds to the impact of your account.

Use clauses to help your reader

I am learning to use clauses to:

→ make my writing interesting for the reader

→ vary the order of information in a sentence for effect

→ include more information in a sentence.

Your writing task

Start by finding out what a clause is and exploring the types. Then try them out by writing a paragraph using different types of clause.
Word count: around 60–100 words
Add annotations to label your subordinate clauses and comment on their impact.

Key terms
Subject: what a sentence is about
Predicate: the part of the clause that provides information about the subject

Activity 1 Identify and write main and subordinate clauses

Each of the sentences below contains a **subject** and a **predicate**.

Subject →	**Davina** came on stage.	← Predicate
	Dermot took the microphone.	
	My friends and I like going to the cinema.	

Each of these sentences could also be called a **clause**. A clause contains a subject and a predicate.

Each sentence above could form an independent **main clause** in a sentence. You can then add a **subordinate clause**. This depends on the main clause to make complete sense:

Davina came on stage, **greeted by wild applause**. ← Subordinate clause

Dermot took the microphone **when it was his turn to speak**.

Subordinate clauses can come before or after the main clause:

Greeted by wild applause, Davina came on stage.

When it was his turn to speak, Dermot took the microphone.

1 Add subordinate clauses before or after these main clauses.

a) The first singer forgot the lyrics

b) The audience cheered

c) The street performers amazed the audience

Activity 2   Identify and use noun clauses

A **noun clause** is one which does the job of a noun in a sentence. It can be the **subject** or the **object**:

> **What I do for a living** (subject) usually disgusts people.
>
> Everyone thinks **that you're very brave** (object).

1 Pair up the noun clauses with verb phrases to make sentences:

Noun clause		Verb phrase
A. what I choose to do		if other people have to suffer
B. he doesn't care		this fingerprint could tell us
C. who murdered Trevor		the voters have made it clear
D. what they want		is none of your business

Activity 3   Identify and use adjectival clauses

An **adjectival clause** adds detail to a noun:

> Dermot, **who is always immaculate**, introduced the first contestant. (Adds to the subject)
>
> I am worried about the weather, **which looks threatening**. (Adds to the object)

1 Rewrite these sentences, adding adjectival clauses where shown.
   a) The newly signed midfielder, …, narrowly escaped being sent off.
   b) The builder shook his head at our roof, …
   c) Kangaroos and koala bears, …, are marsupials.

Activity 4   Identify and use adverbial clauses

An **adverbial clause** does the same work as an adverb: it adds detail to the verb.

> **Until people become perfect,** there will always be crime.
> (Time – when; you could also use connectives like **whenever** and **while**)
>
> **Because Irma couldn't swim,** she sat by the pool.
> (Reason – why; you could also use connectives like **as** and **though**)
>
> People just sit **wherever they want**. (Place – where)
>
> I came **as soon as I could**. (Manner – how)

1 Make sentences by adding adverbial clauses where shown.
   a) …there will continue to be global warming.
   b) …he drank a litre of orange juice in one go.
   c) Nomadic cattle herders wander…
   d) She shouted out…

Activity 5 — Use conditional clauses

Conditional subordinate clauses begin with **if** or **unless**. Here are some examples, with the main clause highlighted:

> If you do as I say, **untold riches will be yours**.
> Unless you leave now, **I will call the police**.

1 Add main clauses to these conditional subordinate clauses to make sentences.
 a) If we could cross the river…
 b) Unless we can escape…
 c) If pigs had wings…

Some conditional sentences have to be reworded to be reversed:

> If the mother cannot feed her cubs soon, they will die.
> The cubs will die if their mother cannot feed them soon.

2 Reverse these sentences.
 a) If the children do not get enough sleep, they will be exhausted.
 b) Unless we find the money, we will have none to spend.

Activity 6 — Hold back the main clause

Sentences can emphasise the key point by holding back the main clause containing the subject:

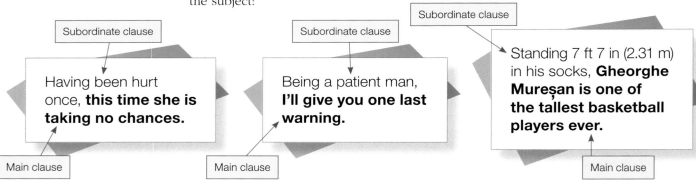

Subordinate clause

Having been hurt once, **this time she is taking no chances.**

Main clause

Subordinate clause

Being a patient man, **I'll give you one last warning.**

Main clause

Subordinate clause

Standing 7 ft 7 in (2.31 m) in his socks, **Gheorghe Mureșan is one of the tallest basketball players ever.**

Main clause

1 Complete these sentences by adding a main clause after the comma.
 a) Having paid attention at school, …
 b) Having no wish to be eaten by alligators, …
 c) Despite being a lover of chocolate cake, …
2 These sentences have the main clause at the end. Complete them by adding a subordinate clause before the comma to add extra explanation or information.
 a) …, I just wanted to go home and get some sleep.
 b) …, she was in a mood for partying.
 c) …, Liverpool is trying to change its image.

Activity 7 Punctuate subordinate clauses

Correct punctuation helps readers to make sense of sentences containing subordinate clauses. Incorrect punctuation can cause confusion, or even a completely different meaning. Compare:

> After eating Alison, Amir and Angela watched TV.
>
> After eating, Alison, Amir and Angela watched TV.

1 Explain the difference in meaning in the following:
   a) I rode the elephant which had huge ears.
   b) I rode the elephant, which had huge ears.
2 Commas are also needed around a mid-sentence subordinate clause. Explain how each of these sentences could mean something different without the commas.
   a) Marlo, who hated arguments, said nothing.
   b) The train, which was full to bursting, pulled out.
3 Rewrite these sentences, adding subordinate clauses in the middle of the main clause, after the subject.
   a) Jamie had apparently come as a pirate.
   b) Esther and Charlene were in charge of keeping the score.

Activity 8 Use subordinate clauses in your own writing

1 Read the extract below about Boxer, a carthorse. Look at the annotations which show how the writer has added detail by using subordinate clauses.

Adds detail using **whose** →

> Nothing could have been achieved without Boxer, whose strength seemed equal to that of all the rest of the animals put together. When the boulder began to slip and the animals cried out in despair at finding themselves dragged down the hill, it was always Boxer who strained himself against the rope and brought the boulder to a stop. To see him toiling up the slope inch by inch, his breath coming fast, the tips of his hoofs clawing at the ground, and his great sides matted with sweat, filled everyone with admiration.
>
> George Orwell, *Animal Farm*, Chapter 6

Adverbial clause of time, showing **when** Boxer did this

Noun clauses showing **what** they admired

2 Write your own paragraph describing one of the following:
   ● a terrifying shark
   ● a prowling cat
   ● a fast cyclist.

Use different types of subordinate clause in at least three sentences. Use the techniques you have learnt in this section and that are shown in the extract above.

3

Know how to vary sentence lengths for effect on your reader

I am learning to vary the length of my sentences to:

→ build tension in narrative for dramatic effect
→ engage the reader by varying pace and creating rhythm
→ persuade my readers using rhetorical effects
→ use word order to show feelings in a story.

Your writing task

Write one or more paragraphs using different lengths of sentence. Start by seeing how other writers have used a variety of sentence lengths. Then try them out in your own writing.

Word count: around 70–100 words

Add annotations to label your key sentences and comment on their impact.

Activity 1 Build tension in narrative

1 Read the extract from *Wolf Brother*, by Michelle Paver, opposite. The author builds tension by using long and short sentences, and even very short paragraphs.
2 What is the effect of the two sentences in the paragraph beginning 'Beside his right boot…'?
3 Michelle Paver could have written:

> Remembering his father's advice to look behind him, Torak spun round, but saw only willow, alder and fir trees, with no sign of a bear anywhere.

How would the effect of this have been different?

Activity 2 Use a variety of sentences in your own writing

1 Write a series of short paragraphs like Michelle Paver's describing someone in a tense situation – for example, thinking they are about to be attacked. Use:
- some long descriptive sentences to set the scene
- a short dramatic sentence to jolt the reader
- a few longer ones to explain
- more short sentences for tension
- some longer sentences for slight relaxation
- short sentence to reach maximum tension.
2 Annotate your writing with comments to show what effects you are trying to achieve (as the annotations on the extract above do).

Focus your effort

Use short, single-clause sentences for dramatic effect, to create tension or to suggest fast action. Don't use too many in a row or they will make your writing seem jerky.

The light was growing, and the air smelt fresh and sweet. Around him the trees were bleeding: oozing golden pine-blood from the slashes the bear had inflicted. Some of the tree-spirits were moaning quietly in the dawn breeze.

Fairly long descriptive multi-clause sentence: relatively calm

Torak reached the stream, where mist floated above the bracken, and willows trailed their fingers in the cold water. Glancing quickly around, he snatched a dock leaf and moved forwards, his boots sinking into the soft red mud.

Another sentence using subordination, but 'Glancing quickly' and 'snatched' suggest fear

He froze.

Instant tension in short sentence: we want to know why

Beside his right boot was the track of a bear. A front paw: twice the size of his own head, and so fresh that he could see the points where the long, vicious claws had bitten deep into the mud.

Look behind you, Torak.

He spun round.

Short, active sentence: more tension

Willows. Alder. Fir.

No bear.

Short paragraphs with very short incomplete sentences – snapshots of what Torak sees

A raven flew down onto a nearby bough, making him jump. The bird folded its stiff black wings and fixed him with a beady eye. Then it jerked its head, croaked once, and flew away.

Longer sentences describing something harmless (but is it?), so we relax a little

Torak stared in the direction it had seemed to indicate.

Dark yew. Dripping spruce. Dense. Impenetrable.

Short incomplete sentences with heavy 'd' alliteration create sense of menace

But deep within – no more than ten paces away – a stir of branches. Something was in there. Something huge.

Sentences get shorter, as if Torak is tense, holding his breath

He tried to keep his panicky thoughts from skittering away, but his mind had gone white.

Longer sentence using coordination, like Torak's thoughts trying to escape?

Activity 3 Vary pace and rhythm for effect using sentence lengths

1 Read the passage below from *Animal Farm*, and see how George Orwell varies sentence lengths to build up a sense of developing action.
2 How does Orwell use short sentences to hold back information in this passage?
3 How does he use sentence lengths in the whole passage to create a sense of the animals' attack on Jones and his men gradually building up?

> The men gave a shout of triumph. They saw, as they imagined, their enemies in flight, and they rushed after them in disorder. This was just what Snowball had intended. As soon as they were well inside the yard, the three horses, the three cows, and the rest of the pigs, who had been lying in ambush in the cowshed, suddenly emerged in their rear, cutting them off. Snowball now gave the signal for the charge. He himself dashed straight for Jones. Jones saw him coming, raised his gun and fired. The pellets scored bloody streaks along Snowball's back, and a sheep dropped dead. Without halting for an instant, Snowball flung his fifteen stone against Jones's legs. Jones was hurled into a pile of dung and his gun flew out of his hands. But the most terrifying spectacle of all was Boxer, rearing up on his hind legs and striking out with his great iron-shod hoofs like a stallion.
>
> George Orwell, *Animal Farm*

4 Write a paragraph of your own, describing action developing and building up to a climax. You could, for example, describe:
   ● a football match or other sporting event
   ● someone knocking over a stall in an open-air market.
Use gradually lengthening sentences to suggest developing action and build to a climax.

Activity 4 | Vary sentence lengths for rhetorical effect

Sentence lengths can be persuasive, especially if they lengthen in threes. Short, single-clause sentences can also have a dramatic effect, for example, suggesting that nothing more need be said.

1 Read the extract below, in which a Native American, Chief Joseph, argues that the US government has no right to confine his people to a reservation.

    a) How does sentence length make 'They are all brothers' powerful?

    b) What is the effect of the next two sentences getting progressively longer?

    c) How does Chief Joseph use two sentences beginning with 'If you …'?

    d) What is the emotional effect of him ending with a long sentence followed by a very short one?

2 Think of something that *you* think is wrong, or feel strongly about, and should be changed. Write a paragraph arguing your case. Use gradually lengthening sentences to build up to one or more climaxes. Finish with a long sentence, like Orwell, or a short, dramatic one, like Chief Joseph.

All men were made by the same Great Spirit Chief. They are all brothers. The earth is the mother of all people, and all people should have equal rights upon it. You might as well expect all rivers to run backward as that any man who was born a free man should be contented penned up and denied liberty to go where he pleases. If you tie a horse to a stake, do you expect he will grow fat? If you pen an Indian up on a small spot of earth and compel him to stay there, he will not be contented nor will he grow and prosper. I have asked some of the Great White Chiefs where they get their authority to say to the Indian that he shall stay in one place, while he sees white men going where they please. They cannot tell me.

Chief Joseph, speech to the US government, Washington DC

4

Know how to order information in sentences to match your purpose

I am learning to vary the order of information in sentences to:
→ change the emphasis of a sentence
→ signal the importance of different pieces of information
→ help the reader to follow a story.

Your writing task

Start by exploring word order as used by other writers. Then try out word order by writing a paragraph in which you use different word orders for effect.

Word count: around 110–150 words

Number of paragraphs: 1–2 Add annotations and commentary to label some of your sentences and suggest what impact your chosen word order has.

Activity 1 Use word order to emphasise different pieces of information

There are several ways to present information in a sentence. You can use different word orders to create different effects, like this:

● Sian picked up the letter and stuffed it in her pocket. (Subject, object, verb phrase: the most straightforward order.)
● Picking up the letter, Sian stuffed it in her pocket. (Starts with a subordinate clause: emphasis is placed on what Sian does with the letter.)
● Sian, after picking up the letter, stuffed it in her pocket. (Uses a subordinate clause between commas: emphasises Sian.)
● The letter was picked up by Sian, who stuffed it in her pocket. (Passive sentence: emphasises the letter – perhaps it is an important piece of legal evidence.)

1 For each of the following sentences, say what is emphasised, and why the writer might have written the sentence in this way.
  a) Just as we thought we were safe, the howling began again.
  b) Debbie spent very little; Lianne, however, was always penniless by pay day.
  c) The chimney was damaged by a storm, the carpet by a winter flood.

2 Read this true account:

> Fellow gang member Robert Ford shot the unarmed Jesse James in the back of the head on 3 April 1882 while James was standing on a chair and dusting a picture.

Key terms
Passive sentence: one in which the subject is acted on by the verb, as in 'The woman was injured by a hit-and-run driver.'
Active sentence: one in which the subject performs the action indicated by the verb, as in 'A hit-and-run driver injured the woman.'

Write new versions, changing the information order, beginning as follows:
a) On 3 April 1882...
b) Jesse James was...
c) While standing on a chair...
d) Robert Ford...

Activity 2 Use word order to signal importance

1 Words appearing at the beginning and end of a sentence usually have more importance. Information near the end often has particular importance. Look at this example:

> Because football is attempting to present itself as a civilised game, despite occasional hooliganism, Liverpool player Suarez has been disciplined for his second biting offence.

a) What is the most important piece of information here?

b) What is the second most important piece of information?

c) What piece of information is least important?

2 Write a sentence of your own following this pattern. It could, for example, be about something in the news, or something that has happened in your school.

Focus your effort

Use active sentences unless you want to achieve a special effect by using a passive one.

Activity 3 Use word order to help the reader when you tell a story

1 Read the following extract. The author has made a number of word order choices.

Sade (pronounced Shah-day) is a Nigerian girl seeking asylum in Britain. She misses Nigeria, and her father, who is still there. She visits a lawyer, Mr Nathan.

Leaning across a wooden desk that looked even more worn than himself, Mr Nathan began by explaining what they would have to do to get permission to stay in England. Sade soon lost track. Asylum, immigration officers, forms, questionnaires, interviews … it all sounded strange and difficult. The desk was as untidy as Papa's, scattered with papers. A forest of books surrounded them, stretching from the floor to the ceiling, while files stacked on the carpet rose up like a thick undergrowth. But instead of the scented pink magnolias outside the window of Papa's study, the rain-stained glass revealed a dense cluster of dull brick and concrete buildings under a drab sky.

Beverley Naidoo, *The Other Side of Truth*

2 Mr Nathan is described as looking 'worn', like his desk, even before the author reports what he says.

a) Why might Naidoo have decided to describe the desk first? What does its appearance suggest?

b) Write your own sentence about someone based on this word order, first describing something significant about the person, then reporting what they say.

3 There are two sentences in which Naidoo mentions 'Papa'.

a) What is the effect of putting him in the first half of each sentence? (Think about how placing can suggest importance.)

b) Write your own sentence like the final one, comparing things you associate with a place you like with a place that you do not like very much.

4 Using your knowledge of how word order can change the impact of sentences, write a description of your impressions of a person on first meeting him or her.

Know how to use cumulative sentences for impact

I am learning to use cumulative sentences to:
- ➔ improve my sentences by adding more detail
- ➔ include more information in a description
- ➔ create emotional impact.

Your writing task

Start by finding out what cumulative sentences are and exploring their uses. Then try them out by writing a paragraph using cumulative sentences.
Word count: around 80–120 words
Add annotations to label your cumulative sentences and comment on their impact.

Activity 1 | Identify and write cumulative sentences

Here are some short sentences:

> The entire front of the building fell into the street.
>
> It roared like an animal.
>
> It sent out a choking dust cloud that billowed out all around.
>
> The rubble enveloped parked cars.
>
> The dust settled to reveal an upper room laid bare like an open doll's house.

These could all be combined in a single **cumulative sentence**, with only slight word changes, like this:

> Roaring like an animal, the entire front of the building fell into the street, sending out a choking dust cloud that billowed out all around, the rubble enveloping parked cars, the dust settling to reveal an upper room laid bare like an open doll's house.

The sentence begins with a descriptive clause: 'Roaring like an animal', followed by the main clause: 'the entire front of the building fell into the street.' It then adds details. This creates a flowing sentence, and gives a vivid impression of all these things happening almost at once – a big, powerful event.

> **Key term**
> **Cumulative sentence:** one based on an independent clause, to which detail is added by several subordinate clauses or phrases, so that meaning accumulates.

1 Rewrite the following sentences to form a single cumulative sentence. You will have to make some changes to the words as you do this. You can change the order of the pieces of information if you wish.
- The peregrine falcon plunged towards the pigeon.
- Its slate-grey wings were folded tightly.
- Its yellow eyes were locked on its prey.
- Its talons stretched out at the last moment.
- It snatched the pigeon out of its flight path.

Each new detail you add in a cumulative sentence could itself have an extra detail added. For example:

> …the dust settling to reveal an upper room laid bare like an open doll's house, a room **in which only that morning people had sat and drunk tea while reading the morning paper**.

Notice that you have to make it clear what the new detail refers to. In this example, the words 'a room in which' do this.

2 Add a different detail to this example, beginning, 'a room in which …'.
3 Add an extra detail to your sentence about the peregrine falcon.

● ●

Activity 2 Add more detail to a sentence to increase its impact

1 Look at this example of a cumulative sentence:

> Alisha drove the white BMW down the country road, her foot hard on the accelerator, the window rolled down, a grim smile on her face, the hold-all containing half a million in used notes sitting on the back seat like a passenger.

a) What is the effect of keeping the detail of the money till last?
b) Write another cumulative sentence based on this one. Begin with a main clause describing someone driving, then add whatever details you like.

● ●

Activity 3 | Include more information in a description

Cumulative sentences can show something happening, but they can also be used to build up a complete description.

1 Read this description of a place in the USA.

The San Bernardino Valley lies only an hour east of Los Angeles by the San Bernardino Freeway but is in certain ways an alien place: not the coastal California of the subtropical twilights and the soft westerlies off the Pacific but a harsher California, haunted by the Mojave just beyond the mountains, devastated by the hot dry Santa Ana wind that comes down through the passes at 100 miles an hour and whines through the eucalyptus windbreaks and works on the nerves.

Joan Didion, *Slouching Towards Bethlehem*

Expand your vocabulary
westerlies – winds coming from the west
Mojave – the Californian desert

a) Using a bullet-point list, summarise the key information on the San Bernardino Valley contained in this single sentence.

b) What three details are given about the Santa Ana wind?

2 Write a cumulative sentence describing a place you know well. You could make yourself the observer, like this:

Rye Lane stretched out before me, the greengrocers selling plantains and coconuts, the Peckham Beauty salon advertising manicures, young mothers pushing pushchairs, their toddlers howling at the traffic ...

Activity 4 | Create emotional impact

Cumulative sentences are often used to give a sense of something big, like a major event, or a broad, spreading scene. They can also be used to create a strong emotional impact.

1 Read this account:

> I would never again set foot on planet Earth, never again walk in the fresh air beside a river on a spring morning, never again hear the sound of birdsong, never again hear the voices of children drifting across from the playground – the playground where I had once played a lifetime ago, where I had made friends who were now lost to me for ever.
>
> Down below me I could still pick out Britain, still see the Atlantic Ocean glinting blue beneath flecks of cloud, still see the outline of Africa, a continent that I had always wanted to visit ... I turned back to the interior of my spaceship, the ship that was to be my home for years to come, the ship in which I might end my life ...

Independent main clause, basis of what follows

Repetition for emphasis

New independent main clause

Repetition emphasises lingering images of Earth

Explain what impression of the writer's feelings is created by repetition and lists in:

a) the first paragraph

b) the second paragraph.

2 Try writing your own cumulative opening sentence like the one above. Imagine that for some reason you will never see Earth, or your home, or friends, or a particular person, again. Begin with an independent main clause and add detail to it, building up to a climax.

3 Add another one or two cumulative sentences to your first one, to make a full paragraph of 80–120 words.

Know how to write concisely, synthesising information using subordination

I am learning to synthesise information in sentences using subordination to:

➜ write informatively but concisely

➜ help the reader by showing the relationships between different pieces of information

➜ help the writing to flow.

Your writing task

Write two paragraphs synthesising information. Aim to use some multi-clause sentences and use subordination.

Word count: around 100–110 words   **Number of paragraphs:** 2

Add annotations and commentary to show how you have effectively synthesised information.

Key term

Multi-clause sentence using subordination: one which has an independent main clause and at least one other clause that depends on it in order to make sense.

Activity 1 | Use subordination in sentences to show relationships between information

1 Rewrite the following sentences, breaking each one down into single-clause sentences. You may have to make slight word changes. How is the impact of the sentences altered by the change?

   a) Backgammon, **which is a game of luck and skill**, is very popular in Turkey.

   b) **Having finished work for the day**, I strolled around the pet shop.

2 Read this group of sentences, about someone climbing the mast of a tall sailing boat at sea to fit a new halyard (a rope to hoist the sails). Rewrite the sentences as a single multi-clause sentence, linking one idea to another in a logical way using subordination.

> The most dangerous thing is falling off. The second most dangerous thing is to be thrown against the mast. I would be wearing a helmet. It would not be difficult to break bones up there.

3 The following groups of sentences continue the account above. Rewrite each group as a single multi-clause sentence using subordination. One way to tackle the first one is to begin with 'As', showing **when** the writer took the mast in her hands and began to climb.

   a) I took the mast in my hands. I began to climb. I felt almost as if I was stepping onto the moon. I had no control over this world.

   b) But it got harder and harder. I was pulling my own weight up as I climbed. I was also carrying the weight of the heavy halyard. It got increasingly heavy. I was carrying nearly 200 feet of rope by the time I made it to the top.

   c) I closed my eyes. I gritted my teeth. I hung on tight. I clenched my wrists together. I hoped.

Activity 2 — Use subordination to allow the language to flow

It is often more enjoyable to read a well-constructed multi-clause sentence than to read several short single-clause sentences, which can seem rather jerky.

1 The following sentences are an account of a stormy boat journey near the South Pole. Read the extract carefully to make sure you understand each one. Then rewrite them as a single multi-clause sentence, using subordination.

> Generally we were upheld by the knowledge that we were making progress towards the land where we would be. Nevertheless there were days and nights when we lay hove to. We drifted across the storm-whitened seas. We watched the uprearing masses of water. They were flung to and fro by Nature in the pride of her strength. Our eyes were interested rather than apprehensive.

Expand your vocabulary

upheld – encouraged
hove to – with the sail rigged so that boat need not be steered, especially in a storm
apprehensive – anxious

2 Read your sentences aloud and consider how they sound compared with the ones above.

Activity 3 — Synthesise information in subordinated sentences in your own writing

1 Write two paragraphs describing a real or imaginary difficult journey. Include two or more subordinated sentences in each. Annotate one of them to show its separate pieces of information.

1 Know how to use commas so your meaning is clear

I am learning to improve my use of commas to:

→ separate items in a list

→ follow an adverb or an adverbial phrase at the start of a sentence

→ mark where a subordinate clause has been used to add extra information.

Your writing tasks

- Write a short description about a place you know well, using at least three sentences and including a list.
- Add an introductory piece of information at the start of a sentence by using an adverb or an adverbial phrase.
- Use commas to show when you have 'dropped in' an additional piece of information, using a subordinate clause.

Punctuation is used by writers to help readers understand what is happening in a text. You need to understand how to use punctuation so that your readers know exactly what you want to convey in your writing.

Activity 1 Use commas to separate items in a list

1 The following extract is from a children's book about the universe. Notice how the commas are used to separate items in a list.

There are no commas in sentences 1, 2 and 3 because they are short and contain only one piece of information or idea.

The universe!

The universe can be a pretty dizzying place. It was born in an almighty explosion of energy. It is almost impossible to imagine how big it really is. Within it, there are spinning planets, burning suns, icy comets and vast clouds of floating dust.

In the last sentence commas are used to separate the different pieces of information: 'spinning planets, burning suns, icy comets and vast clouds of floating dust'.

In a list like this the last item is usually separated from the previous item by 'and'.

2 Read this extract about Earth from the same book, but with all commas removed. Decide where commas should be used to separate the items in a list.

The angry planet

Planet Earth. Third rock from the Sun. 8000 miles wide with a mass of around 6 trillion tonnes. It has forests oceans mountains streams deserts and ice caps. The Earth is home not only to us but also to the billions of other animals plants fungi and bacteria we share it with.

• •

Activity 2 Use commas after an adverb or an adverbial phrase at the start of a sentence

When there is an introductory piece of information at the start of a sentence, it is usually separated from the main part of the sentence by a comma.

1 Read this description about Earth's second moon.

Do we have two moons?

About twenty years ago, astronomers spotted an object about 3 km wide, which was travelling in an orbit not that far from Earth, and named it Cruithne. About ten years ago, they realised it was still with us, sharing our orbit around the Sun, and that it is actually orbiting the Earth. But while the Moon takes just a month to do this, Cruithne takes about 770 years, and it will eventually leave us, flinging away into space for ever.

Key terms

An **adverb** or **adverbial phrase** gives extra information that is usually about one of the following:

- **When** something took place: for example, 'About twenty years ago'
- **Where** it took place: so in this description above the writer could have written 'In an observatory in Chile, astronomers spotted …'
- **How** it took place: so in this description the writer could have written 'After a long struggle, astronomers spotted …'

2 Look at the openings of the first two sentences. The introduction to the first sentence 'About twenty years ago,' tells us when the discovery happened and is separated from the rest of the sentence by a comma. This is called an **adverbial phrase** and gives extra information.

In the first sentence, the extra piece of information 'which was travelling in an orbit not that far from Earth' is separated from the rest of the sentence by commas. The writer has 'dropped in' this extra information into the main sentence. The main sentence would still make sense on its own:

> About twenty years ago, astronomers spotted an object about 3 km wide and named it Cruithne.

The main part of the sentence is called the **main clause**.

The extra piece of information 'which was travelling in an orbit not that far from Earth' does not make sense on its own and is called a **subordinate clause**.

3 From the table below, use commas to add in adverbial phrases at the beginning and subordinate clauses within these sentences describing a climb up a mountain.

a) I set off with my friends to climb to the top of the mountain called Haystacks.

b) We got close to the summit and everyone was really struggling.

c) We arrived at the top feeling really pleased with ourselves.

d) We began the descent taking it in turns to lead the way.

Choose an adverbial to add at the start of each sentence using a comma	Choose a subordinate clause to add to each sentence using commas
Once we had taken photos	where it was quite steep
Finally	whose names are Josh, Karen, Bilal and Jain
After about an hour	which felt much harder than climbing up
Despite the forecast of rain	where you can see amazing views

Activity 3 Use commas in your own writing

1 The next extract describes the way that the Earth's continents were created. Find at least two examples of each of the following reasons for using commas in this extract:

a) to separate items in a list

b) to mark where a subordinate clause has been 'dropped in'

c) to separate the opening information, the adverbial phrase, from the rest of the sentence.

Earth's continents?

Billions of years ago, when the planet was first formed, there was one huge sea, and one massive lump of land, which scientists call Pangea. As the thin crust broke up, Pangea broke up and the pieces drifted apart. Eventually, these pieces became the North American, South American, African, Eurasian (Europe plus Asia), Australasian and Antarctic continents. You can still see evidence of this on a world map. If you look at the east coast of South America and the west coast of Africa, you can see that they fit together, more or less, like pieces of a jigsaw puzzle.

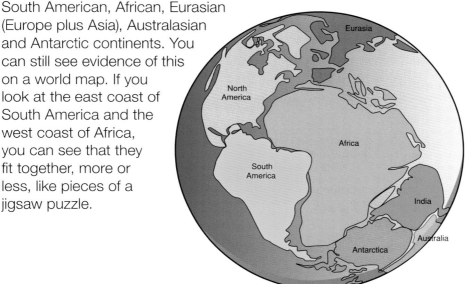

2 Write a short description about a place you know well. Use at least three sentences and include a list. The place might be where you meet with friends or where you play sport or shop.

Remember that the final item in a list usually follows **and** rather than a comma.

3 Add an introductory piece of information at the start of one of your sentences by using an adverb or an adverbial phrase. For example, if writing about sport you could begin with an introduction such as 'If it is a dry day, ...'.

4 Use commas to mark where you have 'dropped in' an additional piece of information, using a subordinate clause. For example, you could add in 'mainly played by boys' or 'mostly played by girls' if you were describing different sporting activities.

Know how to use colons

I am learning to improve my use of colons to:

➜ make my meaning clear to the reader.

Your writing tasks

- Turn information in sentences into a fact file using colons.
- Write a description using colons to introduce quotations.

Key terms

Colons are used to:
- introduce a list
- introduce a quotation or a piece of information
- introduce information in a fact file.

Activity 1 Use colons to introduce a list or a piece of information

A colon is used to introduce a list of items. Here is an example from a guide to an adventure park.

> The park has many brilliant activities for teenagers: Zorb-ball our newest attraction, the thrill-a-minute Mad Trax, quad bikes, archery and clay-pigeon shooting.

Each attraction in the list is separated from the next by a comma

The final item in a list is separated by using **and** instead of a comma

The colon is used to show that the activities will now be listed

A colon is used in a fact file to introduce information. The next extract from the guide gives more information about each activity.

Each activity is followed by a colon which tells the reader that information about the activity follows

> Mad Trax: indestructible buggies, powered by 400cc engines making them fast, really fast!
>
> Zorb-balling: it's the newest, craziest and most exhilarating sport to land in Britain. Bounce, roll and race downhill in our specially created Zorb run.
>
> Quads: a range of high-spec quad bikes with full training and three tracks to ensure maximum thrills and excitement.

The facts about each activity follow the colon. The reader knows that what follows the colon refers to the item before it. So the words 'indestructible buggies' explain what the Mad Trax machines are

1 Write your own fact file of information about a computer game or an adventure or theme park you know.

Activity 2 | Use colons to introduce a quotation

In essays, colons are used to introduce quotations that the writer has selected from the text, as in this extract from an essay about *An Inspector Calls*, a play by J.B. Priestley. Sheila is the daughter of Mr Birling, a factory owner who does not treat his workers kindly.

Sheila shows that her feelings about the workers differ from Mr Birling's views when she says: 'But these girls aren't cheap labour – they're people.' Already, in Act One, Sheila is displaying her thoughtfulness in contrast to her father's views: 'community and all that nonsense'. Birling makes it clear that he doesn't accept responsibility for the people who work for him.

The colon tells the reader that the quotation which follows is something the character Sheila said, demonstrating that her views about the workers in the factory were different from her father's.

Here the colon shows that the following quotation is an example of Mr Birling's views.

1 Write a description of a member of your family or a friend which shows what they are like as a person. Use a colon to introduce a quotation of something they have said.

Here is an example:

My dad always thinks he's so funny and he comes out with many weak jokes: 'You're so slow you'll be late for your own funeral!'

Know how to use semi-colons

I am learning to improve my use of semi-colons to:

→ link sentences without using a conjunction

→ group items together in a long list.

Your writing task

Write a paragraph describing a typical day in your life at school or at home.

- Use semi-colons to link main clauses.
- Use a colon to introduce a list.
- Divide long descriptions in the list with semi-colons.

Key terms

Semi-colons are used to:
- link sentences together without using a conjunction
- group items together in a long list.

> **Activity 1** Using semi-colons to link clauses instead of using a connective such as 'and'

Semi-colons are used to separate main clauses which are linked in meaning without using a connective such as **and**.

Writers use semi-colons because they want readers to make the connection between the two main clauses. In this way a reader is made to think more deeply about the writing. A main clause is complete on its own and can form a complete sentence.

These brief extracts from *Mortlock*, by Jon Mayhew, show the use of semi-colons.

Josie, a magician, has been listening to another magician boasting about his successes to the theatre manager.

The reader first reads that Josie sighs and then thinks about the second part of the sentence and realises that it was the fact that 'she'd heard it all before' that made her sigh. The reader makes these links which helps them engage with the text.

> Josie heaved a sigh; she'd heard it all before.

The main clause after the semi-colon is linked to the first, but the writer uses a semi-colon instead of a connective (such as *because*). This makes the reader think about the links between the two parts.

Later, when the others keep ignoring her Josie shows her disappointment.

The two clauses are both on the same topic: why she is being ignored.

> Josie rolled her eyes. No-one addressed her; it was as if she was invisible.

The semi-colon is used because it makes the reader think about the connection between the two parts.

1 Read these extracts from *The Memory Keeper's Daughter* and note how the writer has used semi-colons to link main clauses.

Caroline has been given a baby to look after but her car has broken down and she is very upset. A lorry driver stops and suggests they sit in his 'rig' (lorry) to keep warm.

> 'Look here, Ma'am,' he began slowly, the steadiness of his voice some kind of anchor. Caroline realised he was being deliberately calm, deliberately soothing; he might even think she was crazy. 'Why don't you come and sit with me in the rig?'

Caroline is now back home and still looking after Phoebe, the baby.

> For the next twenty-four hours, Caroline slept and woke on Phoebe's schedule, staying up just long enough to eat. It was strange; she had always been particular about meals, fearing undisciplined snacking as a sign of eccentricity and self-absorbed solitude, but now she ate at odd hours: cold cereal straight from the box, ice-cream spooned from the carton while standing at the kitchen counter.

Caroline is worried that she is falling in love with the baby even though she is only looking after it for the parents.

> What she had told Lucy Martin was true: she loved looking at this baby. She loved sitting in the sunlight and holding her. She warned herself not to fall in love with Phoebe; she was just a temporary stop.

2 Explain why you think the writer has used semi-colons to link main clauses in these sentences.

Activity 2   Using semi-colons to divide longer phrases in a list

When a list consists of longer phrases, the items are divided by semi-colons, as in the next extract. Here Caroline thinks about the time passing as she waits with Phoebe for her parents to collect her.

The list is introduced by a colon. The reader knows that what comes after the colon will be a list of all the impressions Caroline has experienced.

> For Caroline, the broken days blurred together into a stream of random images and impressions: the sight of her Ford Fairlane, its battery recharged, being driven into the lot; the sunlight streaming through cloudy windows; the dark scent of wet earth; a robin at the feeder.

Because the list consists of longer descriptions such as all the details about the car being returned, the writer uses semi-colons to divide the items in the list.

Activity 3   Use semi-colons in your own writing

1 Now, write your own paragraph, using semi-colons in these ways:
- to link main clauses such as 'My sister was playing her music as loud as she could; Bethany was her usual self.'
- to divide long descriptions in a list.

Use a colon to introduce your list: for example 'I could hear the typical Saturday-morning sounds drifting up the stairs: ...'

Know how to punctuate dialogue for clarity and variety

I am learning to use inverted commas to:

→ punctuate dialogue accurately to show who is speaking.

Your writing task

Write a conversation using inverted commas these ways:

- to interrupt one person's speech with the thoughts of another
- to describe the way a person speaks in the middle of a speech and then write the final words
- to start a person's speech with the way they are feeling so that the reader knows how the speaker says the words.

Activity 1 | Punctuate speech accurately to show who is speaking

The extract below is from *Dead Man's Cove* by Lauren St John. Notice the ways the author shows who is speaking.

Laura is an orphan who has lived in Sylvan Meadows, a children's home, all her life. An uncle has been traced who has agreed to adopt her and Laura is leaving the home to go and live with him.

> Much to Laura's surprise, Matron had been quite tearful at their parting.
>
> 'You'll be sorely missed,' she'd said, standing ankle-deep in snow to give Laura a hug.
>
> 'Really?' asked Laura disbelievingly. She felt a momentary pang. Sylvan Meadows had its imperfections but it was the only real home she'd ever known. The staff were kind and some of them really cared for her. She'd heard horror stories from other girls about Oliver Twist-style orphanages, but Sylvan Meadows wasn't one of them. If she hadn't had big dreams and plans she'd have probably been perfectly content there.
>
> Matron squeezed her hand. 'Hush now. You know Sylvan Meadows won't be the same. You have a spirit about you that's given life to the place. But we'll fear for you. Or at least I will. It's those books of yours. They've filled your head with unrealistic expectations.'
>
> Laura said teasingly: 'What about those romance novels you are always reading with the tall, dark, muscly men on the front? Don't see too many of them around here. Only Doctor Simons with the comb-over and the odd bin man.'
>
> 'That's different.'
>
> 'Why?
>
> Matron smiled thinly. 'That,' she said, 'is one word I won't miss.'

Gives the name of the speaker after the words that have been spoken

Describes the speaker and then allows the reader to infer that this is the person who then speaks

States the name of the speaker before the words they say

Allows the reader to work out who is speaking

Includes the identity of the speaker in the middle of what is said

As only two people are talking here, the reader should be able to follow who is speaking. If there is too much conversation where the writer does not indicate who is speaking, the reader may become confused.

If there are more than two people in a conversation, leaving out the names of the speakers will be very confusing.

1 Now read the next extract, where Laura meets her uncle and his growling dog Lottie for the first time. The speech punctuation in this extract has been left out.
2 Identify where the speech punctuation should go. Remember that speech punctuation is often used for the words a character thinks as well as what they say.

Laura has been driven to her uncle's lonely house by Robbie, the driver from the children's home.

Welcome Laura her uncle said, and that in itself was a head-spin, hearing her name spoken by a person whose blood ran in her veins. For a moment, his whole focus was on her and Laura had the impression of a tall, brooding man with glittering eyes that seemed to see into her soul. A warm hand engulfed hers.

Calvin Redfern he said by way of introduction.

Before she could respond, he'd turned away to greet Robbie. Laura noticed the driver wince as he retrieved his hand.

Can I offer you both a drink? You must have been travelling all day.

Robbie said hurriedly: Thanks, but I have a room booked at the Jamaica Inn near Bodmin. They're expecting me for dinner. His eyes flickered to Lottie who, despite Calvin Redfern's assurances, continued to utter low, threatening growls.

Traitor thought Laura, which she knew was unfair because Robbie was old and had been driving since dawn and still had a long way to travel in the storm. But having wished for this moment for most of her life, she was now desperate to delay it as much as possible.

Robbie put a hand on her shoulder. Laura could see he wanted to give her a hug, but was intimidated by her uncle. Goodbye and good luck, Laura. We'll miss you.

I'll miss you all too, Laura told him, and meant it very sincerely. If she hadn't felt intimidated herself, she'd have run screaming to the car and lain in front of the wheels until Robbie had no choice but to take her back to Sylvan Meadows. As it was she just said: Bye Robbie, thanks for everything.

Activity 2 — Punctuating speech in different ways

In the following conversation between Laura and her uncle, he explains how she should behave now she is living with him. Notice the different ways the speech is punctuated.

Her uncle's request that she follows a rule is interrupted by Laura's thoughts before he continues speaking. This tells the reader she feels he is going to give her a long list of rules. The rest of his speech shows that her first thought was wrong. Breaking up the speech of one character with the thoughts of another character is a useful way to show that character's initial reactions.

Laura's next speech is interrupted by an explanation of how she feels. This explanation helps the reader to realise she will say the final words with real emphasis.

This tells the reader who is speaking but also that he is going to be friendly when he speaks.

'I do have one rule …' he said.

Here we go, thought Laura. I celebrated too soon. One rule will be followed by another rule and then another.

'Actually, it is not so much a rule as a request. I don't believe in rules. It's only this: On no account are you to go anywhere near the coastal path.'

'Why?' Laura asked automatically and could have kicked herself.

'Because it is lonely, goes too close to Dead Man's Cove for my liking, and any number of fates could befall you there,' her uncle responded in a quiet, calm voice that carried some kind of warning in it. 'Humour me.'

'No problem,' Laura said, anxious to show that she was worthy of his trust. 'I'll avoid it like the plague.'

He smiled again. 'Thank you. Now, if you have everything you need, I'll say goodnight.'

'Goodnight,' said Laura, hoping he wouldn't attempt to do something fatherly like give her a hug. He didn't.

When her uncle tells her why she shouldn't go near the coastal path, the way he speaks is explained.

Putting these final words after the description of the way he speaks gives them emphasis and suggests that he pauses before saying 'Humour me.' This is another useful way to vary speech punctuation.

1 Write a conversation between two people using these ways of varying the
   punctuation:
   - Interrupt one person's speech with the thoughts of the other.
   - Describe the way a person speaks in the middle of a speech and then write the
     final words.
   - Start a person's speech with the way they are feeling so that the reader knows
     how the speaker says the words.

   You could:
   - continue the conversation between Laura and her uncle with her trying to find
     out why she shouldn't go near the path
   - write a conversation between you and a friend about a mysterious place.

Know how to use punctuation for effect

I am learning to improve my choice of a range of punctuation so that:
→ my writing has the effect I want on my reader.

Your writing task

Write a blog about a TV programme you have seen. Make it as dramatic as you wish. Use the punctuation you have studied to create effects:

- apostrophes
- exclamation marks
- italics
- capital letters for effect
- ellipses
- dashes
- hyphens
- parentheses.

Activity 1 Punctuate with apostrophes, exclamation marks, italics and capital letters

Read this extract from *The Truth about Leo* by David Yelland. Notice the way the writer uses apostrophes, exclamation marks, capital letters and italics to make the writing clear and create particular effects for the reader.

Leo's father has begun drinking heavily after his wife's death. Leo has to try to keep the truth from neighbours as his father is a very popular doctor. Unknown to Leo, his father has hidden an empty vodka bottle in Leo's school bag and it falls out during a lesson.

> Apostrophes of possession indicate belonging: the floor 'belongs' to the classroom and the bag to Leo.

> Exclamation marks emphasise words and indicate excitement or tension. They lose their impact if used too often. Use them only when you really want to convey a raised voice, or surprise in a character's tone of voice, for example.

> When a writer uses capital letters for a whole word it is often to convey volume or shouting.

> By using *italics*, particularly when writing speech or someone's thoughts, a writer is able to tell a reader that a word is emphasised.

> Apostrophes of omission indicate letters missed out. This is important when writing speech as we often use contractions – words with letters missing – when we speak.

The first Leo knew of the vodka bottle was the loud rolling sound of glass on the classroom's hard wooden floor.

In absolute horror, Leo looked down and saw the bottle with VLADIVOSTI! on the side rolling down the aisle towards the front of the class.

Then he realised. Dad! That was where he'd hidden the bottle. He'd gone and put it in Leo's school bag!

The bottle seemed to be picking up speed as it rolled. Manders was writing on the whiteboard, his back turned to the whole class.

It was rolling towards Manders!

Kids were nudging each other; a murmur started which grew into a loud chatter.

'QUIET!' Manders bellowed. But still his back was turned as he finished writing on the board.

Leo sat paralysed, replaying in his head what must have happened, picturing Dad pushing the bottle into his bag.

It was too late to stand up and snatch it. There was nothing he *could* do.

1 Read the next part of the story where Mr Manders, the teacher, finds the bottle,
   which Leo's friend Flora has hidden in her bag. This time the apostrophes,
   exclamation marks, italics and capital letters for emphasis have been left out.
   Decide where you would change or add punctuation to make the writing effective
   for the reader.

'Silence.' Manders bellowed. He turned back to Flora. 'Open your bag
please. Now.'

The class was still and silent, full of poisoned expectation.

'I said: open your bag' Manders was shouting in her face. 'Come on,
young lady. Open up.'

Flora had begun to sob, her cries the only sound in the hushed class.

It was too much for Leo. Flora had always seemed so grown up to him, so
in charge. But now she just looked like a little girl being bullied.

He stood up and heard himself shouting, almost as if he was somebody
else. 'Leave her alone. Leave her alone.'

And then he was running as fast as he could to the front of the class. With
all the strength he could summon, he pushed Manders away from Flora.

The teacher fell, crashing against the whiteboard. As he fell, Manders
did not say a thing – his face a snapshot of shock, his features frozen by
surprise.

Then Leo was shouting again and he was waving the bottle in the air like
a trophy. 'Its mine, Mr Manders, its mine. Its my bottle – it rolled out of my
bag. She only picked it up. Are you happy now? Are you happy now?'

Activity 2 | Using ellipses, dashes, hyphens and parentheses

1 Notice how the writer uses punctuation for different effects in this extract from *The Truth about Leo.*

Each morning, before Leo goes to school, his father pretends that he wasn't drunk the previous evening and gets ready to open his doctor's surgery. Leo sees their conversation as a game of pretending life is normal.

The dash shows Leo's father pauses while he thinks up an excuse for feeling unwell.

The use of ellipsis shows where the character pauses, perhaps because he is thinking fast and this shows that he is searching for what to say next.

Dashes are used here for parenthesis, an extra piece of information provided in the sentence. Brackets can also be used to show parenthesis.

> Dad paused, scrunching up his face as if something was causing him pain.
>
> 'I guess Mrs York will be here in a jiffy,' he said. 'Tell you what though – I'm not feeling a hundred per cent. Thinking about it … I might get Mrs York to close up the surgery today. She'll be here in a minute, won't she …?'
>
> He watched Dad's eyes, how they darted nervously from thing to thing, always moving, never settling; and never – for as long as Leo could remember – ever looking him straight in the eye.
>
> There was a noise at the door, a key placed in a familiar lock.
>
> A shrill cry from the hall. 'H-e-l-l-o – i-t-s – m-e-e-e …!' This was Mrs York, come to clean, come to scrub, come to help pretend.

At the end of the sentence, ellipsis is used again. This shows that Leo's father can't think of any more to say as he knows Leo doesn't believe him.

Hyphens are used to show the way Mrs York stretches out the words in a silly way to sound cheerful and funny. She knows the truth about Leo's father and has to join in the pretence that all is well. Her silly way of talking helps to do this.

Activity 3 — Write your own description

1 Write a blog about a reality television programme you have seen. In blogs writers often use a range of punctuation to show their strong feelings. Use the punctuation you have studied to create effects:

- apostrophes
- exclamation marks
- italics
- capital letters for effect
- ellipses
- dashes
- hyphens
- parentheses.

Focus your effort

Be wary of using too much punctuation as it will make your writing look over-written!

Know how to link sentences together in paragraphs

I am learning to improve and control my use of sentences in paragraphs:

→ to link ideas throughout a paragraph

→ to ensure my paragraphs show I am moving to the next phase of a story.

Your writing task

Write the opening paragraph of your own story or description. The sentences that follow must link with the opening sentence.

Activity 1 | Why paragraphs are needed

A paragraph is a coherent 'chunk' of meaning or sentences grouped around a common topic or aspect. In narratives, a new paragraph often moves the story on to the next place, time or event. The opening (key) sentence introduces what that paragraph is about.

Any narrative can be broken down into sections. These sections are from the beginning of Chapter 4 of *Harry Potter and the Goblet of Fire*:

1 Harry has packed and is waiting for the Weasleys.

2 The Dursleys are worried about the Weasleys coming.

3 Uncle Vernon asks about the Weasleys' clothes.

4 Harry is anxious about the Weasleys' arrival.

These sections become paragraphs. Each paragraph moves to the next event, time, place, character or speaker.

Activity 2 | Starting a new paragraph

These key sentences in Chapter 4 of *Harry Potter and the Goblet of Fire* introduce the first four paragraphs.

The key sentence opening the first paragraph explains it is the next day, gives the time and says what Harry has done

> By twelve o'clock the next day, Harry's trunk was packed with his school things and all his most treasured possessions – the Invisibility Cloak he had inherited from his father, the broomstick he had got from Sirius, the enchanted map of Hogwarts he had been given by Fred and George Weasley last year.

The second paragraph will describe the atmosphere in the house

> The atmosphere inside number four Privet Drive was extremely tense.

A new, third paragraph is needed for a new speaker

> 'I hope you told them to dress properly, these people,' he snarled at once.

The fourth paragraph is about Harry's feelings

> Harry felt a slight sense of foreboding.

Activity 3 | Add opening sentences

1 Read these paragraphs from the next chapter when Harry has arrived at the Weasleys' house. The opening sentences are missing.

a) Harry recognised it instantly as a gnome. Barely ten inches high, its horny little feet pattered very fast as it sprinted across the yard and dived headlong into one of the wellington boots that lay scattered around the door. Harry could hear the gnome giggling madly as Crookshanks inserted a paw into the boot trying to reach it.

b) To somebody who had been living off meals of increasingly stale cake all summer, this was paradise, and at first, Harry listened rather than talked, as he helped himself to chicken-and-ham pie, boiled potatoes and salad.

c) You really should be in bed, the whole lot of you, you'll be up at the crack of dawn to get to the Cup. Harry, if you leave your school list out, I'll get your things for you in Diagon Alley. I'm getting everyone else's. There might not be time after the World Cup, the match went on for five days last time.'

2 Select the opening sentence below which completes each paragraph.

1) By seven o'clock, the two tables were groaning under dishes and dishes of Mrs Weasley's excellent cooking, and the nine Weasleys, Harry and Hermione were settling themselves down to eat under a clear, deep-blue sky.

2) 'Look at the time,' Mrs Weasley said suddenly, checking her wristwatch.

3) They had only gone a few paces when Hermione's bandy-legged, ginger cat Crookshanks came pelting out of the garden, bottle-brush tail held high in the air, chasing what looked like a muddy potato on legs.

Activity 4 | Paragraphs structuring a description

Paragraphs are also used for each section of a description.

1 Read this opening paragraph.

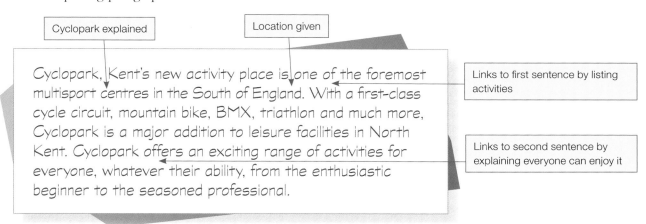

The **key sentence** introduces the subject. The following sentences link with it by providing more information.

2 Read the next paragraph and see how it links to the first paragraph and adds more detail.

Includes information

Second sentence includes more detail

Third sentence covers extra activities

Cyclo-circuit offers a smooth, tarmac circuit 2.9 kilometres long and 6 metres wide, ideal for cycling races, training rides and general fitness cycling as well as skating and running. The circuit can be separated into a number of smaller circuits so whatever the activity or ability, everybody can perfect their skills. From inline skating and competitive wheelchair racing, to slalom skateboarding and adventure racing, the flexible layout means that many sports and competitions will be catered for.

Links to first paragraph describing the 'circuit'

Lists activities

Activity 5 Write a point and include evidence, explanation and exploration

When you are writing about a text, it is important to support each point with evidence. This type of paragraph is often called a PEE (or PEEE) paragraph:

- **P**oint
- **E**vidence
- **E**xplanation
- **E**xploration

You need to make a **point**, give some **evidence** and then **explain** what this shows about the topic. Sometimes an extra **E** is added for **Exploration** – think about or **explore** the ideas.

1 Read this extract from *Dead Man's Cove* by Lauren St John.

After living in an orphanage, Laura has gone to live with Calvin Redfern, a long-lost uncle. On her first morning at his lonely house, Laura meets his housekeeper, Mrs Webb, cleaning her uncle's desk.

A woman with crinkly black hair and a squashed button nose was crouching over Calvin Redfern's desk with a document like a bird of prey about to rip into a mouse. A feather duster lay across a high-backed leather chair.

'I'm cleaning,' declared Mrs Webb, a note of defiance in her voice.

'Of course,' said Laura.

She closed the door quickly and returned to the kitchen, heart thudding. Either her uncle liked his documents polished or Mrs Webb was – what? Going through his personal papers?

2 Now read this example of a paragraph making a point about this extract.

> Laura is suspicious of her uncle's housekeeper, Mrs Webb, from the first moment she sees her 'with a document like a bird of prey about to rip into a mouse'. The simile of a 'bird of prey' shows that Laura feels that Mrs Webb is a dangerous person, like a fierce eagle about to destroy a small mouse. Laura is instantly sure that Mrs Webb is behaving suspiciously and is not a true friend of her uncle's.

Makes a point about the way Laura feels about Mrs Webb.

Uses some evidence from the book in a quotation.

Explains what the quotation shows about Mrs Webb.

Suggests that Laura already thinks Mrs Webb is not a friend of her uncle's. This builds on the explanation and the writer considers how this brief moment affects the story.

3 When Laura sees her, Mrs Webb appears guilty. Choose another quotation from the same passage as evidence for this point. Write the explanation and exploration of what this might mean for Laura.

Start your PEEE paragraph with the point you are making:

> Mrs Webb appears guilty when Laura first sees her.

Activity 6 Write the next paragraph

1 Read this extract where Mrs Webb is suddenly trying to be nice to Laura.

> She purred: 'And how are you finding St Ives?'
>
> 'It's a great town,' said Laura, stabbing her fork into a carrot. 'I really like it here.'
>
> Mrs Webb bared her teeth. 'Well now, isn't that wonderful. And your uncle? You get along with him okay? He has his quirks, that one, but his heart's in the right place.'
>
> 'Oh it definitely is,' Laura agreed, wondering where this was leading.
>
> 'I wouldn't hear a bad word about him,' said Mrs Webb. She added three spoonfuls of sugar to her tea and slurped a mouthful noisily. 'Only …' She moved her chair closer to Laura's. Laura had to make a conscious effort not to push her own away. 'See … I worry about him. It's none of my business but he seems very tired lately.'
>
> You're right, thought Laura. It's none of your business, you old witch.

2 Write a paragraph describing how Mrs Webb is trying to find out more about Laura's uncle. Include a **P**oint, **E**vidence, **E**xplanation and **E**xploration in the paragraph.

Activity 7 Write your own paragraph

1 Now, write an opening paragraph for your own story or a description. Make sure that the rest of the sentences in the paragraph link back to the opening sentence.

Know how to organise and link paragraphs together in a piece of writing

I am learning how to improve and control my use of paragraphs:
➜ to know when to start a new paragraph
➜ to make sure paragraphs link.

Your writing task

Plan and write three or four paragraphs of a comparison of two passages. In each paragraph you must:
- include an opening sentence explaining which part of the comparison the paragraph will be about
- link the opening sentence and the rest of the paragraph.

Activity 1 | Reasons to start a new paragraph

1 There are several main reasons for starting new paragraphs in a narrative. Read these opening sentences from paragraphs in *Harry Potter and the Goblet of Fire*.

- A **new time:**

Lunch was an almost silent meal.

This sentence explains that the story has moved to lunchtime

- A **new place:**

The paragraph is about Harry in his bedroom

Harry spent most of the afternoon in his bedroom; he couldn't stand watching Aunt Petunia peer out through the net curtains every few seconds, as though there had been a warning about an escaped rhinoceros.

- A **new event:**

The Weasleys arrive in an explosion

The electric fire shot across the room as the boarded-up fireplace burst outwards, expelling Mr Weasley, Fred, George and Ron in a cloud of rubble and loose chippings.

- A **new character:**

The paragraph is about Mr Weasley

Tall, thin and balding he moved towards Uncle Vernon, his hand outstretched but Uncle Vernon backed away several paces dragging Aunt Petunia.

- A **new speaker:**

Mr Weasley is a new speaker

'Er – yes – sorry about that,' said Mr Weasley, lowering his hand and looking over his shoulder at the blasted fireplace.

Activity 2 Structure paragraphs in descriptions

In descriptions of places, people or objects, a new paragraph is started for each aspect of the subject.

> Cyclo-terrain is 6 kilometres of mountain bike trails running throughout the park and designed by World Cup trail designer Hugh Clixby. From beginners, to those who thrive on the challenge of adrenaline pumping berms, drop-offs and rock gardens; there is something for all riders as each trail is designed for different abilities.

New paragraph started to describe mountain bike trails

1 Read this section from the description of CycloPark and identify where new paragraphs should begin.

> Cyclo-skate has been planned with local skaters and leading skate-park designers to ensure that it offers a real challenge. At the 1400 square metre Cyclo-skate, skaters of all abilities will learn from each other and the spectator area will be a great place to watch the action. Cyclo-BMX is home to a 330 metre, first-class race track. The use of the BMX track is only during supervised or coached sessions and an induction is required prior to these sessions. The cost of an induction or a supervised session is £5.00. All coaching sessions are priced at £7.00 except beginners' sessions, which are priced at £5.00. Beginners are not permitted to ride supervised sessions. Introducing the new and exciting cyclo-cafe based within the main Cyclopark building. We are delighted to offer our customers a new menu filled with healthy and wholesome snacks and meals. Whether it's a light bite or a main meal, you're bound to find something tasty and enjoyable.

Activity 3 — Describing a person

Descriptions of people or objects also need paragraphs which link together.

1 Read this description and identify how the paragraphs are linked.

Laura Trott is the young British cyclist who won gold at the London Olympics. She was born in Essex in 1992 and was diagnosed with asthma so she took up exercise to help her breathing. She started cycling when her mother took up the sport to lose weight. Laura is a track cyclist and her sister Emma competes in road races.

As a junior, Laura won many races which brought her to the attention of the British team. She won the Junior World Champion title in the Omnium, not to mention winning National titles in track, road and Time Trial racing. The 18-year-old was also selected to compete at senior level in the 2010 European Track Championships and won the gold medal in the Team Pursuit. Laura was also selected for England's Commonwealth Games squad, in which she was the youngest member.

At the Olympics in 2012 Laura was part of the highly successful Team GB. She won gold medals in the Omnium and in the team pursuit with Dani King and Joanna Rowsell. She was made an OBE in 2013.

The description could be organised in other ways such as topics: introduction, a paragraph on her training then a paragraph about her races, and so on.

Activity 4 — Write paragraphs in a comparison

In a **comparison**, the opening sentence of each paragraph explains **which aspect** of the comparison is being covered.

1 Read this scientific paragraph about tornadoes.

The awesome power of a tornado, with wind speeds topping 300 mph, can turn small harmless objects like pencils and pebbles into deadly bullets. These are flung outward from the funnel as it approaches, strafing nearby objects like machine-gun fire. Most tornado injuries come from this flying debris rather than the tornado itself. But if you managed to avoid the debris and enter the funnel, you would be caught in the updraft and flung 100 m into the air along with anything else it picked up. Heavy objects like cars usually land 3 to 6 m away. Clothing and pieces of paper picked up by tornadoes have been known to land over 60 miles away. You would probably land somewhere in between.

Expand your vocabulary

funnel – centre of a tornado
strafing – spraying with bullets from a machine-gun

2 Now read an adult's description of a tornado experienced as a child.

> We were all lying down on the ground, next to a small elm tree. I saw the dog flying in the air, still chained to the dog house. I heard my sister screaming. I saw my dad, bleeding profusely from his head, trying to shield us from the debris. I felt myself being pulled into the wind and I grabbed the little elm tree, hanging on with my little hands. My brother was holding on to the same tree. I remember being lifted off the ground. Then it was total silence and total darkness. Apparently, the trailer had been lifted up into the air, spun around, collapsed like a deck of cards and dropped down on top of us. National Guard Troops managed to find us buried under the rubble of our home.

This is an opening sentence from a comparison of these two passages:

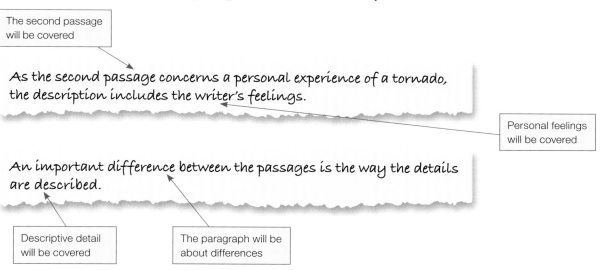

Explains which passage will be covered

The first passage concentrates on providing the reader with facts about tornadoes

Explains that the facts will be covered

Here are two more examples of opening sentences from the comparison:

The second passage will be covered

As the second passage concerns a personal experience of a tornado, the description includes the writer's feelings.

Personal feelings will be covered

An important difference between the passages is the way the details are described.

Descriptive detail will be covered

The paragraph will be about differences

The opening sentence for each paragraph introduces the next part of the comparison.

3 Plan and write three or four paragraphs comparing these two passages about tornadoes. Use the example opening sentences or write your own.

Each paragraph in your writing must have:

- an opening sentence explaining which part of the comparison the paragraph will be about
- links between the opening sentence and the rest of the paragraph.

1

Common confusions

I am learning how to:

→ distinguish quiet and similar sounds in words.

Activity 1 — Hard-to-hear sounds

The way we say words has changed over time, but spelling has been frozen in time. The k in **knight** used to be spoken out loud, for example. There was a time when everyone called a cupboard a **cup board** but it's hard to hear now.

1 Consider how you say:

- handbag (Can you hear the d?)
- discipline (Can you hear the c?)
- gnome (The g is silent.)
- environment (Can you hear the n?)

There are four ways to remember quiet and silent letters:

a) Find a family word in which the letter is clearly spoken. For example:

government – you can hear the quiet n in **govern** and **governor**

definite – you can hear the quiet i in **finite** and **infinity**

b) Look for a base word. For example:

business = busy + ness (the y has changed to i)

handbag = hand + bag (the d came from the base word hand)

c) Say the spelling in full to yourself. For example:

discipline – pronounce the c inside your head when you say this word

parliament – pronounce the i and a inside your head when you say this word

d) Write the word on a card and use a red or highlighter pen to overwrite the quiet letters. Also illustrate that part of the word if it makes sense. For example:

ENVIRONMENT

ENVIRONMENT

Activity 2 How to approach hard-to-hear words

1 Which approach might work for these words?

- separate
- imaginary
- marriage
- believe

Activity 3 Homophones

Many English words share the same sound but have different spellings. Here are some common confusions to learn:

Tip: You eat meat – the clue is the spelling of **eat** and **meat**.

- **Sight**, **site** or **cite**?

Sight = seeing – link **sight** to **light**
Site = building site
Cite = give as an example

- **Have** or **of**?

Have is a verb.
Of is a preposition.
Tip: Could have, should have, would have, might have, may have.

- **Practice** or **practise**?

Practice is a noun.
Practise is a verb.
Tip: Noun endings use **c** and verb endings use **s**. Compare **advice** and **advise**, **prophecy** and **prophesy**.

- **Affect** or **effect**?

Affect is a verb.
Effect is a noun.
Tip: A comes before **e** in the dictionary. The verb **affect** comes before its result or **effect**. Listen carefully to hear the difference.

- **There**, **their** or **they're**?

There = that place
Their = belonging to them
They're = they are
Tip 1: There links with **here** and **where**, all three being about place.
Tip 2: They're is shortened from **they are** and uses the apostrophe to show the missing **a**.

Activity 4 Correct meanings

1 Match these words to their correct meanings.

a) wear   which place
    were   used to be
    where   dress in
b) course   follow a path or route
    coarse   rough
c) brake   short pause
    break   stop the wheels.

Activity 5 Your own writing

1 Collect spelling errors in your own writing that arise from hard-to-hear elements. Find ways to learn the correct spellings.

2

Problem word families

I am learning how to:

➔ get a grip on families of words that contain complex or confusing letter strings.

Activity 1 | The ough family

Many words ending in **ough** say **uff**. For example, **tough**.

1 Think of two more words ending in **ough** pronounced as **uff**.

2 Some **ough** words make a different sound. Try to think of words using these alternative sounds.

Many people find this group of words difficult:

● though – even though
● although – although I know it's a lie
● through – go through this
● thought – I thought about it
● thorough – a thorough job.

They all use the word **though** but these ones add in extra letters:

● **al**though
● th**r**ough
● though**t**
● th**o**rough.

Listen carefully and you can hear the extra letters.

Activity 2 | The igh family

The letter string **igh** is pronounced like **eye**.

1 Go through the alphabet to find the four-letter words ending in **igh**. You should find three.

Activity 3 | The ight family

This is a common letter string but people often get the letters in the wrong order. Learn the correct order and always join up your handwriting when you use this string.

1 Write a list of 10 words ending in **ight**; e.g. **light**. Make sure your handwriting is joined. Feel the movement and remember it.

Activity 4 The ei and ie families

There is a rule which works for most words:

> i before e
> except after c
> or when it sounds like a.

So:

- Most words use **ie**, as in **thief**, **believe**, **field**, **priest**.
- After c, it is usually **ei**, as in **ceiling**, **receive**, **deceive**.
- When it sounds like a, it is often **ei**, as in **vein**, **veil**, **rein**.

There are two useful families to learn:

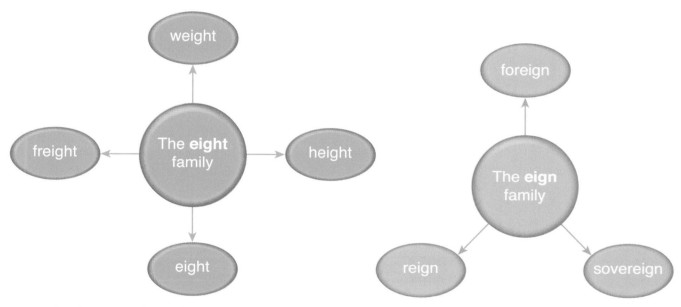

1 Use the clues to work out the missing letters and write the spellings.

great pleasure	del _ _ _ _
near	n _ _ _
sufficient	en _ _ _ _
8	_ _ _ _ _
king or queen	sov _ _ _ _ _ _
respite	rel _ _ f
an idea	th _ _ _ _ _

2 Make sure you learn these important exceptions:

- science
- conscience
- leisure
- protein
- seize
- weird.

3 Sound-alike endings

I am learning how to:
➜ distinguish between similar endings.

Activity 1 | Able and ible

edible		changeable
impossible	BUT	drinkable
horrible		washable

1 Consider why some words end in **ible** and some in **able**. What is the rule?
Clue: Find the base word.

Rule

- If the word has no recognisable base, use **ible**.
- If it is based on a familiar word, you should be able to turn it round, like this: able to drink, able to change, able to wash. In this case, use **able**.

Tip

When you add **able** to words ending in a soft c or soft g, keep the e to keep them soft. For example:

- change – changeable
- notice – noticeable.

Activity 2 | Seed, ceed, cede and sede

1 Consider why these words take the endings they do:

birdseed	succeed	precede	supersede
linseed	proceed	concede	
aniseed	exceed	recede	

TIP
Remember the word SPEED:
S for succeed, **P** for proceed,
E for exceed and **EED** to
remind you of the correct
ending.

Rule

- **Supersede** is the only word ending in **sede**. Learn it.
- **Seed** is used when the meaning is a flower seed.
- **Ceed** is used for three very common words: **succeed**, **proceed**, **exceed**.
- **Cede** is used for all other words and is the most common of these endings.

Activity 3 | Noun and verb endings

1 You have already seen how nouns use c and verbs use s:
- practice (noun)   practise (verb)
- prophecy (noun)   prophesy (verb).

2 Here are some more examples:
- licence (noun)   license (verb)
- advice (noun)   advise (verb)
- device (noun)   devise (verb).

Tip

Use **advice** and **advise** to remember the rule – you can hear the difference in this pair.

Also remember that **ise** is a common verb ending, as in **apologise**, **liquidise**.

Activity 4 | tion, sion or cian (the shun ending)

1 Think of – or look up – five words with each ending: '…tion', '…sion', '…cian'. Can you see any patterns?

Rule
- Use **cian** for words ending in **ic** such as **magic**, **politics**, **mathematics**, **optics**.
- **tion** is the most common ending.
- **sion** often appears in words ending in **d** or **s**.

2 Think of other, less common ways of spelling the **shun** ending. Do you see any patterns or rules for using them?

3 Pick out the correct spelling from these lists.

a) extension	extention	extencian
b) mathematision	mathematision	mathematician
c) succeed	succede	sucseed
d) examination	examinasion	examinacian

Building on roots

I am learning how to:
→ recognise the roots in words
→ understand how words are built up using prefixes and suffixes.

Activity 1 — Base, prefix and suffix

The **base** word is the one at the heart of a spelling when you strip away the added-on parts.

A **prefix** is an addition to the front. A **suffix** is an addition to the end.

Here are two examples:
- **unproductive:** base word – **produce**; prefix – **un**; suffix – **ive**
- **disgraceful:** base word – **grace**; prefix – **dis**; suffix – **ful**.

1 Identify the base word in:
- defrosted
- anticlockwise
- reaction
- nightwatchman
- prehistoric.

Activity 2 — Ancient roots

Many base words and prefixes come from Latin or Greek:

bi = 2	aqua = water	anti = against
tri = 3	mater = mother	cide = kill
oct = 8	pater = father	circ = round
cent = 100	bio = life	audi = hear
mar = sea	vis = see	pod/ped = foot

1 Think of three words to illustrate the use of each root above. Check that these letter strings still carry the ancient meaning in your words. For example, **martial** has no link with the sea.

Activity 3 | Prefixes

1 Work out the meanings of these common prefixes.
- **re** as in revise, replay, rewind
- **pre** as in prepare, pre-order, prevent
- **post** as in posthumous, posterior, postscript
- **de** as in decamp, deconstruct, defuse
- **extra** as in extraterrestrial, extraordinary, extricate
- **trans** as in transport, transfer, transition

Activity 4 | Suffixes

Many suffixes change the meaning of the word. Sometimes they make the base word into a verb, and sometimes into an adjective, noun or adverb. Sometimes they change the tense of a verb.

1 What changes are brought about by these endings to the base word **garden**?
- gardener
- gardening
- gardened
- gardens

2 What do these endings commonly do to a base word?
- **ise** as in liquidise
- **er** as in farmer
- **dom** as in kingdom
- **ness** as in kindness
- **ly** as in slowly
- **ify** as in justify
- **ate** as in agitate
- **ish** as in foolish

3 Work out the meaning of these words, using their roots:
- matricide
- biodiversity
- tripod
- submariner.

Use this approach to crack unfamiliar words. Work back from words you do know.

Know how to improve your grammar

1 Standard English

I am learning to use standard written English to:

→ communicate clearly and accurately.

Standard English is the form of the English language which is found in books, magazines, newspapers and other media. It is a form of English that isn't associated with any particular region of the country, and is widely accepted as being clear and proper English. When you write using Standard English, the rules are agreed so that anyone can follow what you mean.

To use standard written English:

- Choose a more formal vocabulary. Avoid colloquial, dialect, non-standard or swear words because they may not be understood or appreciated by your reader.
- Make sure your nouns and verbs 'agree'.
- Use the standard form of verbs, especially the verbs **be**, **have**, **go** and **do**.
- Use the standard pronoun (for example, make sure you get **I** and **me** the right way round).
- Remember to put **ly** on the end of adverbs.
- Choose the English rather than the American word. Also be aware that Americans spell some words differently.

Activity 1 | Use a more formal vocabulary

1 Choose a more formal expression for:
- grab a bite
- his mum
- down in the mouth
- got into uni
- a bit cold outside
- unreadable
- turned up late.

2 Which words need to be changed or dropped in this formal application? Write out a more formal version.

> I'm dead interested in the job because I sort of enjoy working with animals. I think vets are great. I enjoyed biology at school and I got a B in my GCSE. I have tons of pets at home such as a dog, a cat, a guinea pig and a parrot.

Activity 2 — Use the standard form of the verb 'to be'

The verb 'to be' is the most common verb and it should be used in this way:

I am	I was
you are	you were
she is	she was
he is	he was
it is	it was
we are	we were
they are	they were

The verb 'to be' is a tricky verb because it has three unique endings in the present tense and two endings in the past tense. Even so, many regions use an everyday version of 'to be' which has different endings, as in these examples of non-standard use:

We is walking by the canal.

He were a good teacher.

We was well-pleased.

These are fine for local use, when you are talking, but are not appropriate in standard written English.

1 Choose the correct form of the verb 'to be' in these cases:
   ● We was / were bored.
   ● I am / is / are going to bed.
   ● I wasn't / weren't there.
   ● She ain't / isn't / aren't interested.
   ● You is / are / am a good friend.
2 Draw and fill in a table like the one below for the verbs:
   ● have
   ● do
   ● go.
Consider whether there are local versions to bear in mind.

	Present	Past
I		
you		
she		
he		
it		
we		
they		

Activity 3 | Use rules for agreement

Agreement means consistency between nouns and verbs. It is an important part of standard English. If a noun is singular, the verb must also be singular; if a verb is singular, the noun must be singular. If one is plural, so must the other be.

Consistency in writing is important. Check that you keep to the same tense, the same gender and the right pronouns. Readers will be confused if you mix them.

1 Identify the problems here and explain what is wrong exactly. Then write a version that agrees.
   a) The boy often choose team sports and they enjoyed them.
   b) Girls are more successful in art than a boy.
   c) Girls tend to be good at English and boys were better at maths.

2 Which sentence in these pairs is the correct standard written English? Explain why.
   a) Five pounds is a lot of money.
      Five pounds are a lot of money.
   b) No one is happy about a rise in bus fares.
      No one are happy about a rise in bus fares.
   c) The council was divided on the introduction of a wind farm.
      The council were divided on the introduction of a wind farm.
   d) Four metres of cloth is enough to make the dress.
      Four metres of cloth are enough to make the dress.
   e) Everyone needs to be loved.
      Everyone need to be loved.
   f) The class is making good progress.
      The class are making good progress.

Rules for agreement

Money and measurements are usually treated as singular, so the correct Standard English is:

Five pounds is …	Four metres of cloth is …

Collective nouns are treated as singular. There is only one council and only one class, so:

The council was …	The class is …

No one and everyone are singular. The clue is the word 'one'. So:

No one is …	Everyone is …

3 Work out whether the following should take a singular or a plural verb:
   a) all of us
   b) nobody
   c) the staff (in a school)
   d) ten hours.

4 Write down the correct version of the words in bold in this letter.

Dear Ms Janelta,

Thank you for **agreement** to visit our school. Everyone **are** excited about your visit and your kind offer **to be singing** your new release. It isn't often that an ex-pupil **have** succeeded in the competitive world of pop music. The governing body **have** also asked me to pass on **their** thanks. We are all very much **look** forward to your visit.

Yours sincerely,

Tina Turner

Headteacher

Activity 4 | Understand subject and object

Here is the main group of pronouns:

| I | you | she | he | it | we | they |

These pronouns are used when the pronoun is the **subject** of the sentence. This means that it is the focus of the sentence, and is usually the 'doer' in the sentence. The subject often comes near the beginning of the sentence, like this:

> **We** look for the best in other people.
>
> **She** is the best singer in the group.
>
> Every night, **they** play at the computer.

When a pronoun is not the subject of the sentence, but its **object**, the word may change. For example:

> Give the pen back to **him**.
>
> He disliked **her**.
>
> They called **us** the next day.

When these pronouns are the object of a verb, they become:

| me | you | her | him | it | us | them |

Notice that five of the pronouns change when they are on the 'receiving end' of the sentence and not its main subject. Notice also that they come later on in the sentence in the examples above.

Advice for using pronouns

- Pronouns can save repetition by replacing a noun.
- The noun has to be introduced first.
- Don't overuse the same pronoun – it sounds clunky and repetitive.
- It helps if you stitch sentences together.

1 Rewrite this paragraph, including the words 'the twins' once only, and the pronoun 'they' just twice.

> The twins waited for the rain to stop. The twins sheltered under a tree. The twins waited twenty minutes. The rain did not stop. The twins began to walk home in the rain.

Tip: It helps to join up some sentences.

Activity 5 | Use pronouns correctly

You can use pronouns in your writing in place of a noun that you have already introduced.

Pronouns avoid the need to repeat the noun over and over again. Look at the following example:

> Jon missed the bus. Jon had to walk home. Jon took a short cut through the estate. Jon arrived home only ten minutes late.

You can replace most of the names (Jon) with a pronoun (he), but even so, it will be a clunky paragraph:

> Jon missed the bus. He had to walk home. He took a short cut through the estate. He arrived home only ten minutes late.

The repetition of 'Jon' has been replaced by the repetition of 'he'.

You can try stitching sentences together to reduce the repetition of pronouns, like this:

> Having missed the bus, Jon walked home. He took a short cut through the estate, and arrived home only ten minutes late.

Activity 6 | Noun and pronoun

When a noun and a pronoun are linked (e.g. Mary and I), they are either joint subjects of the sentence or joint objects. For example:

Joint subjects of the sentence

Jahmeel and I walk to school together.

The teacher gave the gym key to me and Jahmeel.

Joint objects of the sentence

1 Choose the correct pronouns and write out the sentences.

a) I / Me asked they / them to help pick up litter.

b) Mrs Jones and I / me carried the litter bags out to the bins.

c) The headteacher gave we / us an extra half hour to tidy up.

When pronouns are used as adjectives:

- **I** changes to **my** –   Give me back **my** pen.
- **You** changes to **your** –   It's not **your** decision.
- **We** changes to **our** –   That is **our** house.

2 Work out what happens to these pronouns when they are used as adjectives:

- she
- he
- it
- they

2 Formality

I am learning to adapt my language so that I can:
→ write in a more formal way.

Formality is a key part of Standard English. There are degrees of formality. You would find **very formal** language used in a court of law. You would find **formal** language at an interview. But you might, in discussion with your teacher, adopt a more **relaxed formality**.

Features of formal sentence grammar:
- It is impersonal.
- It is often expressed in the passive voice.
- It uses nominalisation.

Activity 1 | Impersonal sentences

A **personal sentence** says who did what. The action is done or seen through the eyes of an individual, and so it is personal. A personal sentence says what people think, feel and do.

An **impersonal sentence** does not mention the people who do the actions. The doer is much less important; even pronouns disappear. An impersonal sentence tries to be neutral, like a statement of fact. It contains facts, observations and neutrality.

Here are some examples of personal and impersonal sentences:

The boys at our school love to play computer games. (Personal) Computer games are a favourite pastime of many schoolboys. (Impersonal)

I don't know who burgled the house. (Personal)
The identity of the burglar is unknown. (Impersonal)

Many people enjoy holidays in Cornwall. (Personal)
Cornwall is a popular holiday destination. (Impersonal)

1 Turn these personal sentences into impersonal sentences:
- Most of them choose to study biology.
- About half of us in school prefer to bring in a lunchbox rather than have school dinners.
- My classmates and I like chemistry better than physics.
2 Turn these impersonal sentences into personal sentences:
- Music is more popular with boys than girls.
- Dukinfield has a population of 15 000.
- The early closure of the shop is inconvenient and unwanted.

Activity 2 | Use the passive voice

Formal sentences often use the **passive voice**. When an active sentence is rewritten as a passive sentence:

- The object of the active sentence goes first (and becomes the subject of the passive sentence).
- The verb is altered to say what happened to the new subject (rather than who did what).
- The doer (the agent) in the active sentence sometimes disappears altogether.

An **active** sentence tells you who did what to whom:

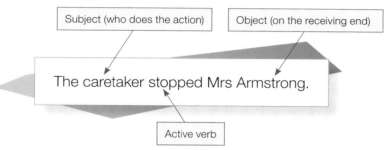

A **passive** sentence turns it all round:

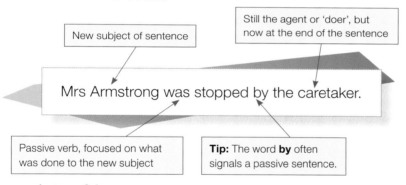

Notice the reordering of the sentence:

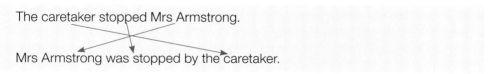

The order is reversed in the passive. Here is another example:

The dog bit the man's ankle. (Active)
The man's ankle was bitten by the dog. (Passive)

1 Turn these sentences into the passive:
- Ghulam laid the table.
- Palaentologists have discovered a new dinosaur in Utah.

2 Turn these sentences into the active:
- The meal was prepared by Ghulam's father.
- Sheena was cared for by the school nurse.

Activity 3 | Removing the agent

Many formal sentences are also passive sentences because the passive voice plays down the role of the 'doer' (known as the **agent**). Sometimes they leave out the agent altogether.

Example A

The secretary mislaid the money. (Active)

The money was mislaid by the secretary. (Passive)

The money was mislaid. (Passive without the agent)

Example B

The police stopped the speeding car. (Active)

The speeding car was stopped by the police. (Passive)

The speeding car was stopped. (Passive without the agent)

Example C

The lab assistant combined the acid and the copper sulphate. (Active)

The copper sulphate was combined with the acid by the lab assistant. (Passive)

The copper sulphate was combined with the acid. (Passive without the agent)

There are several reasons to remove the agent:

- To avoid blaming someone (e.g. the secretary in Example A).
- Because it's obvious who did it (e.g. the police in Example B).
- Because it doesn't matter much who did it (e.g. the lab assistant in Example C).

1 Change these active sentences into **a)** the passive and **b)** the passive without the agent.

- The council raised local taxes.
- The milkman delivered the wrong number of milk bottles today.
- Henry VIII closed and plundered the monasteries.

2 Change these passive sentences into the active.

- The bank was robbed by a gang.
- The rider was thrown from his saddle by the horse.
- The First World War was triggered by the assassination of a prince in Sarajevo.

Activity 4 — Use nominalisation

Another feature of formal language is **nominalisation**. This means making a noun out of a verb, or an adjective. For example:

> We all eat because it is good for us. ('Eat' is a verb.)
> Eating is good for us. ('Eating' is a noun here. It means the act of eating.)

> The students collected £70 for charity. ('Collected' is a verb.)
> The collection raised £70 for charity ('Collection' is a noun.)

> The problem was that the cross-country course this year was too long. ('Long' is an adjective.)
> The length of the cross-country course this year was a problem. ('Length' is a noun.)

Like the passive voice, nominalisation avoids saying who did what. It removes the agent.

1 Nominalise the words in bold to make these sentences more formal.

- We were late for our meeting because the train **departed** 20 minutes late.
- The invaders **constructed** new roads enabling fast communication between towns.
- We are not allowed to **run** in the corridors.

2 Use what you know about formal vocabulary, the passive voice and nominalisation to find at least five features of formality in this paragraph.

Learning outside the classroom used to be seen as a treat for 'good' children. It was considered 'time off'. The fact that pupils enjoyed it was seen as evidence that it was not serious learning. Today, a different view is taken. The outdoors provides opportunities to study geography, science and other subjects in action. Textbooks have been exchanged for first-hand experience. The smallest pond holds a wealth of resources for the biology teacher because it is a mini-habitat with mini-creatures in it. The benefits for pupils include seeing the objects of their studies in context and in real time. Outdoor learning areas have been built inside the grounds of many schools so that all pupils can benefit from first-hand study.

Sophistication

I am learning how to:

→ make my writing voice sound more sophisticated.

Four ways to write in a more sophisticated style are:

- to vary the starts of sentences
- to subordinate more clauses
- to vary the order of clauses
- to streamline writing to make it more fluent and coherent.

Activity 1 | Varying the starts of sentences

If you write at length but use only one sentence structure your writing can sound plodding and repetitive. An easy way to break this style is to start sentences in the middle of the action by saying how, why, when or how the action takes place.

Examples of 'when' openings

In the middle of the night	Later that day	Meanwhile

Examples of 'where' openings

Further up the road	Down in the cellar	In a nearby café

Examples of 'why' openings

Tired of waiting	Unable to sit still any longer	Surprised by the noise

Examples of 'how' openings

Without a second thought	Running at full speed	Slowly

All these openings are **adverbials**. They add to the verb and tell the reader more about the action. Some are single words (like 'Slowly'); these are **adverbs**. Others contain a string of words and are **adverbial phrases** or **clauses**. Together, they are all known as **adverbials**.

Notice the comma after each one. When you move an adverbial to the beginning of the sentence, it is usual to put a comma at the end of it.

1 Move the adverbials to the beginning of these sentences. Don't forget the commas.

- I went to see Neil at about one o'clock.
- I rushed over without thinking.
- Neil welcomed me with his lopsided smile.

2 What effect does this move have on the information that is in each sentence?

3 Invent adverbials for the beginning of these sentences. Don't forget the commas.

- I told him I was really angry with him.
- He asked me why I was angry.
- I found it difficult to put my feelings into words.

Activity 2 | Use different grammatical structures for starting sentences

There are several different starting patterns for your sentences. You can start with:

- an adverb, e.g. Slowly …, Reluctantly …
- an adverbial phrase, e.g. After Danny left …, With a sudden lurch …

- a present participle (an **ing** verb), e.g. Shouting …, Leaving …
- a past participle (an **ed** verb), e.g. Exhausted …, Humbled …

1 Rewrite this paragraph to sound more sophisticated by including two or three different ways of starting a sentence. Combine sentences if you wish; that will make it less repetitive.

> It was a long hike. I was aching by the time we reached the hostel. I collapsed into an armchair because I was exhausted. Marian was undeterred and proposed that we all walk back again. I was amazed. I told her that I admired her energy but I was staying put.

Look at this example:

| Main clause | Subordinator | Subordinate clause |

Anji will not go to the disco unless one of her friends goes with her.

'Anji will not go to the disco' makes sense on its own but 'unless one of her friends goes with her' makes little sense without the main clause.

You could rewrite the example above like this:

Unless one of her friends goes with her, Anji will not go to the disco.

Notice that:
- The subordinate clause has moved to the beginning, but it is still the subordinate clause.
- The main clause has moved to the end, but it is still the main clause.
- The subordinator has moved with the subordinate clause and now starts the sentence.
- **Important:** A comma has been added to mark the start of the main clause. It acts as a buffer between the main and subordinate clauses.

Changing the order of clauses can help if the focus of your attention lies in the object or receiving end of the sentence. Perhaps you want to focus on the victim or outcome of an action, and therefore put it later in the sentence. Small afterthoughts usually come last, but if you want to emphasise a reservation or quibble, it helps to put it where it gets more attention.

Here are some examples:

> Putting aside her principles, Kate agreed to buy the cigarettes.
> Though he knew they were bad for him, David smoked them.
> Unsurprisingly, he developed a smoker's cough.

Activity 3 Use subordinate clauses

1 Rewrite each sentence, moving the subordinate clause to the beginning of the sentence:
- Lola agreed to go with Anji, even though she did not much enjoy discos.

Key terms

Clause: a simple expression with a noun and a verb. It can be a complete sentence.

Main clause: just what it says – the main part of the sentence and the focus of attention. It can stand alone and still make sense.

Subordinate clause: a helper clause. It helps the main clause and cannot stand alone. It depends on the main clause for its meaning.

Subordinator: first word of a subordinate clause; tells you how and why the subordinate clause is related to the main clause. It acts as a kind of warning that a subordinate clause is about to appear. Examples: unless, despite.

- The school sports day took place on the last day of term as it always did.
- Sports day was well attended despite the pouring rain.

2 Check your answers. Did you remember the buffering comma each time?

Activity 4	Putting the subordinate clause in the middle of a main clause

A subordinate clause can sometimes be moved to the middle of the sentence, like this:

> She ran for shelter under the trees **when the rain started to fall**.

> She ran, **when the rain started to fall**, for shelter under the trees.

Notice the use of two commas to act as buffers between the main and subordinate clauses.

1 Move the subordinate clause to the middle of this sentence:

Marie knew that her mother was not fit to work, without really understanding why.

2 Move the subordinate clause to the front of this sentence:

She was able to help out with chores after she got home from school.

3 Move the subordinate clause to the end of this sentence:

Her mother was back home, feeling very much better, after a brief stay in hospital.

4 Revisit some of your recent pieces of writing and consider where and how you might have improved your sentences by varying their structure.

Streamlining

One of the features of mature writing is that it is economical, confident and expressed in a mature style. It isn't plodding. It isn't simplistic. It sounds grown-up.

Making your writing more streamlined will involve:
- lengthening sentences by joining clauses
- making better use of pronouns
- editing out wasted words
- better stitching together of ideas by using connectives.

Activity 5	Lengthening sentences by joining clauses

Lengthening sentences by joining clauses is different from lengthening sentences by adding more detail. It means pulling together linked ideas so that the reader sees the connections.

This paragraph is broken by too many full stops; its sentences are too short and it sounds childlike because nothing is linked:

> Jay's first day had started with an assembly. Then there were lessons. There was science. Then there was maths. Then there was English. Then it was lunchtime. Lunchtime was an hour long. There wasn't much to do. Jay found it dull. Then there was French and then there was history. Jay liked the teachers. He thought the lessons were interesting. He didn't make any friends.

1 Try rewriting this paragraph by grouping sentences together so that you end up with four or five.

- Pay attention to the way you join sentences. Avoid using too many 'and' joins which will sound just as clunky.
- Try to subordinate some clauses, or condense them into a single sentence.
- Consider starting your sentences in different ways.

You could begin:

> In the morning, Jay attended an assembly and lessons in science, maths and English …

Activity 6 | Make better use of pronouns

Avoid repetition by using **pronouns**.

1 Revise the paragraph below using the names Jay and Ahmed **twice only**. Look for ways to use pronouns such as 'he' and 'they' or expressions such as 'the other boy' instead.

It will help if you join sentences together to avoid having to re-introduce your subject over and over again.

Take care!
Use pronouns only when it will be clear to the reader who you mean. As this paragraph is about two boys, check that your reader will know who 'he' refers to.

> On his second day, Jay sat next to Ahmed in his first lesson and they worked well together. Jay liked Ahmed. Ahmed was shy but he was also clever. Jay also sat with Ahmed in his second science lesson and they discovered that they shared an interest in astronomy. Jay also joined Ahmed in the dinner queue at lunchtime. Jay liked Ahmed and they soon became great friends.

Activity 7 | Edit out wasted words

Repetition can be effective to make a point, but it is often a waste of words. You can abandon repetition and condense into one sentence, like this:

> There was science. Then there was maths. Then there was English.
> There was science, English and maths. (Condensed)

1 Condense these overloaded sentences into one:
- Jane's favourite lesson was biology. Her second favourite lesson was English. Her third favourite lesson was PE.
- Manny was bored that Saturday morning so decided to walk into town. He walked two miles to get there. He bought a notebook at the newsagent's.

1 Know how to choose words precisely

I am learning to choose words to match my purpose so that I can:

➜ be precise in my meaning

➜ use a wider vocabulary

➜ make use of word associations.

Your writing task

Write one or more paragraphs using well-chosen words for a particular purpose. Then try them out in your own writing.

Word count: around 100–150 words   **Number of paragraphs:** 1–3

Add annotations and commentary to label some of your sentence types and suggest what impact they have.

Focus your effort

Many words are close to other words in meaning, yet do not mean exactly the same thing. Try to choose words that express the exact meaning you intend. If in doubt, use a dictionary.

Activity 1 · Choose words that express your meaning precisely

1 Choose from the options to complete the news report sentences below. Use a dictionary to check on exact meanings if necessary.

   a) The police officer was convicted of using … force in arresting the suspect. (outrageous / excessive / extreme)

   b) As an … monument, Stonehenge is protected by law. (antiquated / antique / ancient)

   c) The confidence trickster's business suit was always … (immaculate / beautiful / untarnished)

   d) The judge said Kray was a … criminal who cared nothing for his victims. (cruel / callous / menacing)

   e) The defence claimed that Smith was stupid rather than …: she had never meant any harm. (horrible / evil / malicious)

   f) Evans said that the medication made him feel …: 'I just couldn't summon up any enthusiasm for anything.' (apathetic / idle / lethargic)

2 Choose three of the words you did **not** use in Question 1, and use each one in a sentence to express its meaning.

Activity 2 · Use words to write more concisely

You can often write with more impact by being more concise – replacing several words with one or two. For example:

Lucinda's behaviour in assembly was **shockingly bad** (appalling).

1 Replace each of the phrases in bold with the most accurate single word from the list below. Use a dictionary to check meanings.

a) My hay fever was **made worse** by walking through the long grass.

b) The MP was met by the **loud and insistent** cries of protesters.

c) He is a **person who claims to be virtuous and criticises others for faults he has himself**.

d) The huge mudslide **completely buried** the village.

e) The boy looked **as if he was trying to hide something**.

f) She was executed for being a **person who had supported her country's enemies**.

traitor	aggravated	engulfed	furtive	vociferous
hypocrite	booming	villain	drowned	timid

2 Rewrite the following expressing the phrases in bold more concisely:

> These people **are deserving of the whole country's admiration for their courage**. They should be **held in high esteem**, not **treated as if they didn't exist**.

Activity 3   Use word associations

The words used to describe or label something, or somebody, can have a powerful effect on the reader's attitude. In particular, words can have **positive** or **negative** associations.

1 In the passage below, George Monbiot describes kayaking at sea. What words or phrases tell us whether this was a positive or negative experience for him?

> A moment later a bull bottlenose dolphin exploded from the water, almost over my head. As he curved through the air, we made eye contact. If there is one image that will stay with me for the rest of my life, it is of that sleek gentle monster, watching me with his wise little eye as he flew past my head. I have never experienced a greater thrill, even when I first saw an osprey flying up the Dyfi estuary with a flounder in its talons.
>
> *Guardian, 1 June 2009*

2 The following words could all be used to describe the same person in a news report. Put them in order, from most positive to most negative.

terrorist   rebel   freedom-fighter   radical   activist   revolutionary   murderer

3 a) Write a sentence comparing the meanings of the most positive and most negative words in your ranking. Explain what ideas you 'associate' with these words.

b) Now do the same for two words that are closer to each other in your ranking.

4 Write a description of a real or imaginary person or experience. Use language concisely, and choose words to make your account **either** positive or negative. For example, you could describe someone accused of a crime either in a positive way, as if you were defending this person, or in a negative way, as if you were prosecuting.

Know how to choose and sustain register and tone

I am learning to use register and tone so that I can:

→ judge how formally to write for a particular purpose
→ write with an appropriate level of formality
→ choose a tone in which to communicate with the reader
→ write consistently in the tone I choose.

Your writing task

Write an account in a register and tone of your choice. Find out what register and tone are, then try them out in your own writing.

Word count: around 60–100 words

Add annotations to label your word choices and comment on their impact.

Activity 1 — Judge how formally to write for a particular purpose

You would use a **formal** register (style of language) in a serious news report, or in a job application. You would use an **informal** register when writing casually to friends, in writing in which you want to be more playful, or if you want to sound friendly and helpful.

1 On a scale of 1 to 5, if 1 is informal and 5 is formal, rate the following writing purposes:

a) a will (as in 'Last Will and Testament')

b) a short article in a magazine for teenage girls, 'Friday Fitty – Danny O'Donaghue!'

c) a leaflet on 'How to Care for Your Hamster'

d) a travel brochure on holidays in the Costa del Sol (Spain)

e) a Facebook message to a friend challenging them to an online game.

Activity 2 — Identify formal and informal language

1 Read the two pieces of writing opposite.

a) Decide which is **less** formal, and explain how you can tell. Think about the types of sentences, the choice of words, and the tone in which the writing speaks to the reader.

b) Make a two-column table of formal and informal writing features like the one begun below. Fill in features based on the texts opposite.

Formal writing features	Informal writing features

c) Explain in a short piece of writing why you think the formal or informal register is appropriate for each text.

Starspot Your daily horoscopes... decoded!

Taurus 21 April – 21 May

Mates

Your mates have been, well, pretty flamin' amazin' recently, so it's time to make sure they know how much they mean to you … Big birthday day out? Yep, we think so, too!

Dates

You've been crushing on the same guy for aaages, but he doesn't seem to be taking the hint. Time to take a deep breath and take the plunge – even if you only speak to him on the bus, it's still a step forward!

Lookin' Great

Trend alert: You might not know it, but you've got cheekbones to die for! But how can anyone see your gorgeous bone structure if you don't make the most of it? We prescribe lashings of peachy blusher!

Shout magazine online, May

I was now five, and still I showed no real sign of intelligence. I showed no apparent interest in things except with my toes – especially those of my left foot. I used to lie on my back all the time in the kitchen or, on bright warm days, out in the garden, surrounded by a family that loved me and hoped for me and that made me part of their own warmth and humanity. I was lonely, imprisoned in a world of my own, unable to communicate with others, cut off, separated from them as though a glass wall stood between my existence and theirs. I longed to run about and play with the rest, but I was unable to break loose from my bondage.

Then, suddenly, it happened! In a moment everything was changed, my future life moulded into a definite shape, my mother's faith in me rewarded and her secret fear changed into open triumph.

My Left Foot by Christy Brown

---

2 Arrange the sentences in these groups of three in order of formality, from most formal to least formal.

a) I am seeking accommodation. I'm on the lookout for a place to kip. I'm trying to find a place to stay.

b) You must be gutted! You have my deepest sympathies. What a pity.

c) He was not entirely trustworthy. He was a bit of a dodgy character. He was a man of questionable integrity.

3 a) Write a formal invitation to an event, and then write a very informal one.

b) Write a sentence or two explaining how your two invitations differ.

What do you know about… the author?

Christy Brown was a writer and artist who was born with cerebral palsy. *My Left Foot* is his account of growing up and living his life unable to control any part of his body other than his left foot.

Activity 3 | Identify and choose a tone

Tone in writing is like the 'tone of voice' in which someone speaks. You could speak, or write, in many different tones: angry, friendly, cold, gushing, sinister, and so on. This is the 'mood' of the writing.

Tone also suggests the kind of relationship that the writer wants to create with the reader, and the kind of response that the writer wants to get. For example, a writer may want readers to take a text seriously, or to be amused.

1 Read the two extracts opposite, and see how their language creates tone.

2 Which of the two authors do you think wants to be taken more seriously? What language features make you think this?

3 Compare how the use of statistics in each extract affects the tone.

Activity 4 | Use tone in your own writing

1 Word and phrase choices can strongly create a particular tone, like the word 'laughable' in the newspaper article. What tone might be created by using the following words and phrases to describe someone's behaviour?
   a) a bit naughty
   b) not cool
   c) completely unacceptable
   d) bang out of order
   e) contemptible.

2 Consider the following phrases used to describe bullying in school. What tone does each suggest?
   a) the most pressing issue in education today
   b) just one of those things
   c) an amusing pastime for the bullies, but less so for the bullied
   d) a despicable expression of the lowest human character traits
   e) a process of natural selection – the survival of the fittest.

3 Write an account giving your own views on one of the following:
   ● social-networking sites
   ● reality TV shows.

   Use language that consistently creates a recognisable tone.

Bill Bryson compares Britain with America

Irony: Bryson knows perfectly well there are no moose in Britain

Very casual language

Consider this: every year in New Hampshire a dozen or more people are killed crashing their cars into moose. Now correct me if I am wrong, but this is not something that is likely to happen to you on the way home from Sainsbury's. Nor are you likely to be eaten by a grizzly bear or mountain lion, butted senseless by buffalo, or seized about the ankles by a seriously perturbed rattlesnake – all occurrences that knock off a few dozen hapless Americans every year. Then there are all the violent acts of nature – tornadoes, rockslides, avalanches, flash floods, paralysing blizzards, the odd earthquake – that scarcely exist in your tranquil little island, but kill hundreds and hundreds of Americans every year.

Finally, and above all, there is the matter of guns. There are 200 million guns in the United States and we do rather like to pop them off. Each year, 40 000 Americans die from gunshot wounds, the great majority of them by accident. Just to put that in perspective for you, that's a rate of 6.8 gunshot deaths per 100 000 people in America, compared with a meagre 0.4 per 100 000 in the UK.

America is in short a pretty risky place.

Bill Bryson, *Notes from a Big Country*

Does he really care as little as his language suggests?

Irony: as if we don't have **enough** gunshot deaths

Attack of the vapers

News Insider online editorial November 2013

Why is this word in quotes?

Suggests that as e-cigarettes become more popular, their use will become more acceptable

New behaviours often pose etiquette problems and the sudden popularity of e-cigarettes is challenging society's assumptions about where it is appropriate to 'smoke' (or rather, 'vape') More than a million people are using them in the UK and, according to Bloomberg, on present trends they will outsell conventional cigarettes by 2047. So is it now OK to 'spark up' in an office, restaurant or train carriage?

Critics warn that e-cigarettes risk glamorising smoking among the young and could act as a gateway to the real thing. This is as laughable an argument as the idea that brightly coloured cigarette packaging 'encourages' children to start smoking. Both arguments are utter rubbish, of course.

In fact, e-cigarettes offer liberation from the deeply unjust constraints placed on smokers by the smoking ban. E-cigs have no smell, making them more acceptable for use in social situations, and because they contain few toxins offer a safer nicotine-delivery system than real cigarettes. Plus, they are a powerful aid to smokers who want to quit. 93% of people who try to stop smoking using nicotine patches or gum fail within the first twelve months. To these people, e-cigarettes offer a more satisfying alternative.

Viewpoint expressed by dismissive phrase

Positive emotive word choice

Negatively emotive phrase

Know how to get across a point of view

I am learning to improve my use of language so that I can:

→ choose strong, persuasive language
→ use emotive language
→ back up my arguments with factual details
→ use words and phrases that help the reader through my arguments.

Your writing task

Write a letter to your MP expressing your views on a local issue.
Word count: around 90–120 words
Add annotations to label your key sentences and comment on their impact.

Activity 1 Choose strong, persuasive language

You can express a point of view in a simple statement, such as 'I think that school should finish at lunchtime on Fridays', or you can use language to suggest the same view:

> Verb choice suggests slowness

> The little hand points to 3, and the big hand crawls to a vertical position – which is more than most of the yawning pupils could do as this dreary Friday afternoon drags to a close.

> Adjective and verb suggest boredom or tiredness, using alliteration

> Revealing detail

1 Try this yourself.
   a) Write a simple statement expressing your point of view – real or made up – on any subject.
   b) Now write a sentence expressing the same view without using 'I think' or 'should'.
2 Now write a sentence about something you think is good – such as a band, or something you enjoy doing. Again, avoid using 'I think' or 'should'. Underline the words that especially make this a positive sentence.

Activity 2 Use emotive language

Emotive language aims to get an emotional response. It can be serious, as in charity appeals, or it can use a lighter approach to express a viewpoint.

1 Read the extract opposite. Some emotive language is annotated. Explain the effect of the other phrases in bold.
2 List three other examples of amusingly negative language that Jan Moir uses for Alan Sugar and his contestants. Comment on the effect of each example.
3 In paragraph 3 Jan Moir mentions the contestants' 'anonymity'.
   a) What point is she making?
   b) How does she use language to make it?
4 Write three paragraphs criticising a TV show. Use similar techniques to those of Jan Moir.

I can't take any more of these sad, deluded wannabes

Suggests an unruly lower-class mob who are vain and talentless

Like a film character witnessing a terrible accident

It is painful to watch

The BBC1 series, which features the liverish Sir Alan Sugar as mentor and benefactor to a rabble of hopeless show-offs, is back for a ninth series next week. Nooooo! For how much longer can this torture lurch on?

The format is now more threadbare than Sugar's noggin, with little more than six million viewers tuning in to last year's final. That is the lowest audience since the show was upgraded from its niche slot on BBC2 to a prime-time BBC1 showcase in 2007.

What has gone so horribly wrong? I blame the ever-decreasing quality of the **crummy contestants**. A decade on from the first series and every single one of them appears to have **sunk back into the swamp** of success-free anonymity — with the exception of 2010 winner Stella English.

Earlier this year, she hit the headlines again when she sued Sir Alan for constructive dismissal — and lost.

I can't think of a single one of the self-styled Apprentice hot-shots who has gone on to make a huge success of their business lives, can you? A situation which, apart from stretching our credulity, kind of makes the whole thing **a lame waste of time.**

Sir Alan is right when he says he has not let any budding Mark Zuckerbergs or Richard Bransons slip through his sausagey fingers. Which suggests the wannabes who sign up for it are invariably the same kind of self-serving attention-seekers who couldn't stack a shelf after attending a six-month shelf-stacking course.

Do they really think appearing on a show like this is how to make it in business? Or are they just madly deluded?

This year's crop includes Luisa, a cupcake shop owner — there's an original business idea! — from St Albans, who says she has 'the sex appeal of Jessica Rabbit and a brain like Einstein'.

We all know, don't we, that it is going to be the other way around.

Jan Moir, Mail Online, 3 May 2013

Expand your vocabulary

liverish – irritable

Activity 3 | Support your arguments with factual details

To write persuasively, you have to back up your arguments with detail. You also have to choose effective language to express that detail.

1 Read the two extracts opposite. Which do you find more convincing? Explain why you have decided this.
2 Make a table like the one begun below, showing the main arguments of the two extracts.

Dea Birkett	Benjamin Zephaniah
Trainers really care for animals.	Circus animals are like slaves.

3 What details or evidence are used to back up these arguments?

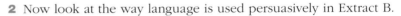

Activity 4 | Use positive and negative language

1 Look at the way language is used persuasively in Extract A.
  a) What words or phrases in the first and last paragraphs give a positive view of having animals in the circus?
  b) What phrase makes training animals seem innocent and normal?
  c) How does Birkett back up her argument in paragraph 4 ('Animal behaviourist …')?
  d) What language in paragraph 4 makes the argument convincing, and how does it do this?

2 Now look at the way language is used persuasively in Extract B.
  a) What phrases suggest that Zephaniah is especially qualified to write on this subject?
  b) What particularly negative words and phrases are used to criticise the use of circus animals in paragraph 1?
  c) What verbs are used to show how animals are treated, and what is their effect?
  d) What adjectives are used to show how this treatment affects the animals, and what is these adjectives' effect?

Activity 5 | Write your own persuasive text

1 Imagine that a circus that uses trained animals is coming to your area. An animal activist group plans to disrupt it on the grounds that using animals is cruel.
  a) Plan your main points for a letter to the council **either** defending the circus **or** agreeing with the activists and asking for the circus to be banned.
  b) Write your letter using persuasive positive or negative language and details like those used in the two extracts.

Extract A

'Cruel? No, elephants love the circus – and I should know', says Dea Birkett, 'I used to ride them in the Big Top'

Daily Mail, 25 February 2009

In the circus, the lives of the humans and the animals are completely entwined. No other people live so closely with the animals they care for. And it's the welfare of the animal performers, not the humans, that always comes first.

Julia* hadn't been plucked from the jungle or captured in an elephant trap. Almost all circus animals are born in captivity. And many animals we think of as wild are considered domestic in the rest of the world. In India, elephants are seen in the same way as we consider horses – they're working beasts.

And what's wrong with training animals to perform? It is no different from training a racehorse or teaching the family dog to respond to 'Sit!' at the kerb.

Animal behaviourist Dr Marthe Kiley-Worthington, who was commissioned by the RSPCA to report on animals in circuses, says many animals enjoy being taught tricks. After 3000 hours of scientific observation, she concluded it was wrong to assume animals should always be kept in a primitive, natural state.

Just as some human beings, such as athletes and circus artistes, enjoy tackling new physical skills, so do some animals. Even an old dog can learn new tricks.

***Julia** the elephant that the author used to ride in the circus

Extract B

Animals in circuses: a modern-day slave trade, Benjamin Zephaniah

Guardian, 30 November 2012

My Jamaican heritage and African roots make it impossible for me to ignore the historical similarities between cruelty to my own ancestors and cruelty to animals in circuses today. The mindset that has permitted atrocities to be inflicted on humans is the same mindset that allows the abuse of animals to occur. Just as my ancestors were beaten and exploited, so are the zebras, lions, tigers, camels and other animals used in circuses. Just as my ancestors had families, feelings and emotions, so do animals. In fact, when

I strip away the material stuff around me, I see that I, too, am an animal. We are family.

Treated as if they were equipment, animals who are forced to travel and perform in circuses are routinely deprived of proper care and become sick, listless and depressed. Many develop neurotic behaviour from the stress and abuse and die far short of their expected lifespan. They spend the vast majority of their lives crammed into transport cages or boxcars and are hauled around from one venue to the next.

Know how to use rhetorical techniques for effect on your reader

I am learning to use rhetorical techniques so that I can use:

→ triples to drive home a point
→ repetition to reinforce an argument
→ lists for effect
→ parallel sentence structures for effect.

Your writing task

Write a speech using a range of effective rhetorical techniques. Find out what these techniques are, then try them out.
Word count: around 120–150 words
Add annotations to label your techniques and comment on their impact.

Focus your effort

Speak your sentences aloud to see if they really work. They should be grammatically correct and flow rhythmically.

Activity 1 Use triples (triads) to drive home a point

There is a sort of magic in making a point with a list of three words or phrases:

> I came; I saw; I conquered.
>
> (Julius Caesar)

1 What phrase does Barack Obama use three times in his first paragraph opposite?
2 Imagine you have been made World President. Write an opening paragraph for your victory speech in which you promise the world three things. Introduce each one with a repeated phrase.

Activity 2 Use repetition to reinforce an argument

1 Deliberate repetition can be powerful.
   a) Why does Obama repeat 'answer' in his victory speech? Suggest possible reasons.
   b) What words does Hillary Clinton repeat in her speech opposite? With what effect?
   c) What phrase does Martin Luther King repeat? What is the effect?
2 Continue your victory speech, adding one or more sentences using repetition. Refer to world problems that you intend to tackle.

Activity 3 Use lists for effect

1 Find Obama's list of the range of Americans supporting him.
2 Add to your victory speech a list of the kinds of people you will help – or bring to justice!

Activity 4 | Use parallel sentence structures for effect

Parallelism is repeating a phrase or grammatical structure, but with a key change, as in Martin Luther King's 'the sons of former slaves and the sons of former slave owners'.

1 How does King use parallelism in his final paragraph? With what effect?

2 Use parallelism to add one or more sentences to your speech telling your supporters what a contrast there will be between the old world and **your** world.

Barack Obama's speech on becoming President of the USA

If there is anyone out there who still doubts that America is a place where all things are possible; who still wonders if the dream of our founders is alive in our time; who still questions the power of our democracy, tonight is your answer.

It's the answer told by lines that stretched around schools and churches in numbers this nation has never seen; by people who waited three hours and four hours, many for the very first time in their lives, because they believed that this time must be different; that their voices could be that difference.

It's the answer spoken by young and old, rich and poor, Democrat and Republican, black, white, Hispanic, Asian, Native American, gay, straight, disabled and not disabled – Americans who sent a message to the world that we have never been just a collection of individuals or a collection of Red States and Blue States: we are, and always will be, the United States of America.

Hillary Clinton speaks to Fourth World Conference on Women

I want to speak for those women in my own country, women who are raising children on the minimum wage, women who can't afford health care or child care, women whose lives are threatened by violence, including violence in their own homes. I want to speak up ... for women who are working all night as nurses, hotel clerks, or fast-food chefs so that they can be at home during the day with their children.

Martin Luther King speaks in Washington DC, 1963

I have a dream that one day on the red hills of Georgia, the sons of former slaves and the sons of former slave owners will be able to sit down together at the table of brotherhood.

I have a dream that one day even the state of Mississippi, a state sweltering with the heat of injustice, sweltering with the heat of oppression, will be transformed into an oasis of freedom and justice.

I have a dream that my four little children will one day live in a nation where they will not be judged by the colour of their skin but by the content of their character.

Know how to use different sorts of simile

I am learning to use different sorts of simile so that I can:

→ use similes using 'like'
→ use similes using 'as' and 'than'.

Your writing task

Write a description using all three types of simile. Find out what they are, then try them out.
Word count: around 80–100 words
Add annotations to label your similes and comment on their impact.

Activity 1 | Use similes using 'like'

A **simile** is a kind of word picture, also known as a **figure of speech**. It brings something to life by comparing it with something that is similar in at least one important way, but different in others. Here is an example:

> A rugby player since childhood, Davies had legs **like** oak trees.

1 Complete these sentences with similes of your own:
   a) The excited fans swept across the pitch like …
   b) The jet passed overhead with a sound like …

A simile can also describe something abstract:

> Becoming Prime Minister is like climbing a greasy pole.

Notice that although 'becoming Prime Minister' is something abstract, it is compared to something in the physical world.

2 Think of similes using 'like' to complete these sentences:
   a) Love is …
   b) When you're alone, fear can be …

Sometimes a simile comes with an explanation:

> Life is like a box of chocolates: you never know what you're going to get.

3 Think of explanations for these similes:
   a) Hatred is like acid: …
   b) Memories are like autumn leaves: …

Activity 2 | Use similes using 'as' and 'than'

One common type of simile identifies the similarity between two things:

> Her skin is **as soft as** rose petals.

This is a simile of quantity or extent.

1 Think of similes like this to complete the following:
   a) She'll be fine: she's as tough as …
   b) They were as lively as …

Focus your effort

Some similes become **clichés**: they become stale through overuse. An example is 'as black as night'. In writing it is more effective to use original similes. Even adding a word or two to a cliché can improve it: 'as black as a moonless night'.

You can take this technique further by using 'than', perhaps with exaggeration:

She moved faster **than** a rattlesnake.

2 Think of similes to complete the following:
  a) Her smile was wider than …
  b) It's hotter than … in here.

Activity 3 Use similes that really fit what they describe

The most effective similes fit what they describe in more ways than one.

1 Suppose you're writing a story about a rugby game and you want a simile to complete the following:

  Dale had the ball, but the entire Pontypool scrum were bearing down on him like …

  So, what would the Pontypool scrum seem like to Dale at this moment? A concept map or spidergram could help

  a) Think of some options. For example, buses are powerful and heavy, but not usually out of control or muddy.

  b) Choose from your options. What simile would work best?

2 Use the same technique to find similes using 'like', 'as' or 'than' to complete the following:
  a) I fell under the hypnotist's spell …
  b) Derek was just one puny little human, facing a giant …
  c) The bride flitted from one guest to another …

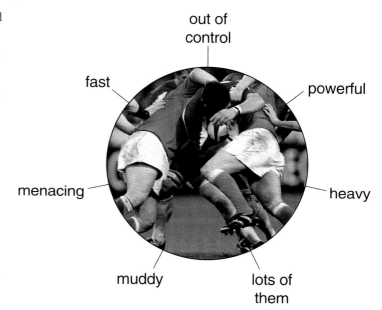

out of control

fast

powerful

menacing

heavy

muddy

lots of them

Activity 4 Write your own description using similes

1 Read this opening to a novel:

> Taller than a house, the Iron Man stood at the top of the cliff, on the very brink, in the darkness.
>
> The wind sang through his iron fingers. His great iron head, shaped like a dustbin but as big as a bedroom, slowly turned to the right, slowly turned to the left. His iron ears turned, this way, that way. He was hearing the sea. His eyes, like headlamps, glowed white, then red, then infra-red, searching the sea.
>
> Ted Hughes, *The Iron Man*

2 a) Find the similes in this extract.
  b) Explain how each simile is effective.
3 Write your own description of a mysterious creature, being or person using at least one of each type of simile. Use some of Ted Hughes' ideas if you wish.

Know how to use metaphors and personification

I am learning to use metaphors and personification so that I can:

➡ create vivid images
➡ bring ideas to life
➡ express feelings about a subject.

Your writing task

Write a description using metaphors and personification. Find out what they are, then try them out.
Word count: around 80–100 words
Add annotations to label your metaphors and personification and comment on their impact.

Activity 1   Use noun phrase metaphors

A **metaphor** is a word picture that brings something to life by describing it as if it is something else that is similar in at least one way, but different in others. One type of metaphor uses a noun or noun phrase:

> The Jamaican nurse Mary Seacole was a **beacon of hope to the wounded soldiers**.
>
> You are **a brick wall over which I must climb in order to succeed**.

Notice that these metaphors simply say that the subject is or was something else. They imply a comparison without using 'like'.

1 Add noun phrase metaphors to these sentences:
  a) The thugs were … closing in on their victim.
  b) To African village children, education is …
  c) Freedom of speech is …

Activity 2   Use verb metaphors

1 A metaphor can also take the form of a verb. What comparison is implied by each of these verb metaphors?
  a) Andrea Bagley rocketed to fame after winning *The Voice UK*.
  b) Your words pierced my heart.
  c) Do you ever feel like just burrowing under the duvet?
2 Make up sentences including verb metaphors to describe someone who:
  a) is trapped by their own self-pity
  b) comes into a room quickly, angrily and unexpectedly
  c) is bright and lively at a party.

Activity 3   Use noun phrase and verb metaphors together

1 It can be effective to combine both types of metaphor:

> Some celebrities swim happily in the tropical ocean of fame; others are hermit crabs that scuttle out of the limelight.

  a) Find the verbs that describe the behaviour of the two types of celebrity.
  b) Explain how noun phrases are used to make comparisons in this example.
2 Think of three pieces of advice to young people. Each must include a noun phrase metaphor and a verb metaphor, like this:

> Swim boldly in life's great ocean!

Activity 4   Use personification

A **personification** describes an abstract thing or idea as if it were a person, animal or god:

> Disease and Famine follow on the heels of War. (Like dogs following their owner.)
>
> The wolves of hunger howl outside the poor man's door. (Starvation threatens the poor.)
>
> Love blesses us with her gifts. (Like a goddess bestowing blessings.)

1   Think of ways to complete these personifications:
   a) The many-headed monster of hatred …
   b) Self-doubt tries to tell us that …
   c) Death, the grim reaper …

Activity 5   Use metaphors and personification to express feeling

1   Read these extracts and notice how the authors use metaphors and personification to express feelings about their subjects.

> It was a very narrow street – a ravine of tall, leprous houses, lurching towards one another in queer attitudes, as though they had all been frozen in the act of collapse. … My hotel was called the Hotel des Trois Moineaux. It was a dark, rickety warren of five storeys, cut up by wooden partitions into forty rooms.
>
> George Orwell, *Down and Out in Paris and London*

> Having leprosy – unhealthy place

> Unstable, crowded; people living like rabbits

> How they look to people outside when lit up

> The Fairy palaces burst into illumination, before pale morning showed the monstrous serpents of smoke trailing themselves over Coketown. A clattering of clogs upon the pavement; a rapid ringing of bells; and all the melancholy mad elephants, polished and oiled up for the day's monotony, were at their heavy exercise again.
>
> Charles Dickens, *Hard Times*

> Sinister personification for pollution

> Strange metaphor for industrial machines

2   Write a description of your school at one or more particular times of day. What does it look like and sound like? What about the students? Use metaphors and personification to make your description come alive. Choose them to express a feeling or viewpoint.

Know how to use sound effects

I am learning to use sound effects so that I can use:

➡ alliteration and assonance for effect
➡ onomatopoeia to make writing more vivid
➡ rhythm to enhance meaning.

Your writing task

Write a poem using sound effects. Find out about them, then try them out.

Word count:

around 60–80 words
Add annotations to label your poem to comment on its sound effects.

Focus your effort

Judge your sound effects by the effect they have on you when you read the words aloud. For example, a hard c (or k) sound gives a harsh impression, as in 'Cousin Cora was callous and cutting.'

Activity 1 Use alliteration and assonance

Alliteration is the use of repeated consonant sounds (not a, e, i, o, u), usually at the beginnings of words:

> **S**eason of **m**ists and **m**ellow **f**ruitfulness,
> Close bosom-**f**riend of the **m**aturing **s**un

Here John Keats uses alliteration to make autumn sound soft and harmonious.

1 Write a line about something you find restful and relaxing. Use soft-sounding alliteration to emphasise the mood.

2 **a)** What alliteration can you find in these lines by Shakespeare?

> All's cheerless, dark, and deadly.
> Your eldest daughters have fordone themselves,
> And desperately are dead.

Expand your vocabulary

fordone – committed suicide

b) Say the lines aloud. What effect does the alliteration have?

c) Write one or more lines about something dark, deadly or desperate using alliteration in this way.

3 **Assonance** is the repetition of vowel sounds. It is usually less obvious than alliteration:

> Hear the mellow wedding bells.

a) Here the writer Edgar Allan Poe uses assonance to create a sense of harmony, and to suggest bells ringing. What sounds does he repeat?

Here is another example:

> How I long to hear the howling owls.

b) Write one or more lines like this using alliteration and assonance together.

Activity 2 Use onomatopoeia

Onomatopoeia is hard to spell, but fun to use! It means the use of words that echo the sound they describe.

Some easy examples are:

> oink   ding-dong   miaow   quack

Less obvious are:

> **tinkling** bells   **crashing** waves   **splashing** water

1 **a)** Make a spidergram of examples for sounds you might hear in your home.

   b) Choose some of your words to write a short poem of 4–5 lines describing these sounds. It need not rhyme. It could begin with 'Clinking cutlery …'

Activity 3   Use rhythm

Rhythm is a musical quality. It helps to create the right mood, and it often directly echoes the meaning of a poem.

1 Here is the start of Tennyson's poem 'The Charge of the Light Brigade'. Read it aloud, thinking of galloping cavalry:

> Half a league, half a league
> Half a league onward,
> All in the valley of Death
> Rode the six hundred.
> 'Forward, the Light Brigade!
> Charge for the guns!' he said:
> Into the valley of Death
> Rode the six hundred

Expand your vocabulary

half a league – about one and a half miles

2 Write an eight-line verse using this rhythm. You could, for example, copy Tennyson's rhythm but write about a football team, or yourself in the third person. For example:

> Emily, Emily
> Ran for the school bus …

Activity 4   Use sound effects in a poem

1 Write a poem using all the sound effects you have looked at in this section: alliteration and assonance; onomatopoeia; and rhythm. Choose one of these topics for your poem:

- one of the four seasons
- sights and sounds in your home (add smells if you want!)
- a sports event
- your favourite things.

You can use any of the lines you have written so far if you wish.

Know how to choose and sustain voice

I am learning to choose and sustain a narrative voice so that I can convey character using:

→ first-person narrative
→ an 'unreliable narrator'
→ the third person as an all-knowing narrator
→ the third person from one character's viewpoint.

Your writing task

Write a story using the **voice** of your choice. Find out about the different voice options, then try them out.

Word count: around 200–350 words

Add annotations to label your story to comment on how you have used voice.

Activity 1 | Use first-person narrative

You can use a first-person narrator to tell a story using 'I', 'me', 'my'. This can make the story seem very vivid and immediate. As the narrator tells the story, they can express something of their own character.

1 Read the extract from *The Baby and Fly Pie* opposite. It is from the first chapter, so it is still giving the reader some background before the real action starts. Fly Pie, an orphan who lives by scavenging on rubbish dumps, describes how he once found a diamond ring.

The author **shows** the character of the narrator, Fly Pie, by what he describes himself doing, and what he thinks. He does not just make Fly Pie **tell** us what he is like.

2 Discuss what Melvin Burgess reveals about Fly Pie. Then make a table like the one below.

Character trait	Evidence
Clever enough to keep a secret	'I didn't tell.'

3 Imagine you are a 'rubbish kid', or another person very different in character and situation from the real you. Write a paragraph in the first person, in the voice of this character. Try to reveal two or three main character traits.

4 Swap your paragraph with a partner.
   a) Read each other's paragraph and try to find the character traits revealed.
   b) Check to see if your partner agrees with the character traits you identified in their paragraph.

Finding treasure

I found treasure once. It was a ring
with diamonds in it. The diamonds
were tiny but they were real. They
cut glass, which everyone knows
is a good test for diamonds.
Actually, they were quite big for
diamonds but I only found that out
later on.

I found the treasure in a little cloth
bag. I just put my hand in and felt
it and I knew at once. I took it out,
I had a quick look to see if it really was treasure and then I put it straight
in my pocket. I didn't tell. I went on going through the rubbish and I never
said a word. Later, when I was on my own, I had a good look at it. You
find bits of jewellery quite often and most of it isn't worth much, but I
scratched the window at the back of an old warehouse with this ring and
then I knew it was real.

I kept the ring in my pocket for a few days while I wandered about
the dealers, the antique shops, the jewellers, comparing prices. I was
planning on selling it and setting up for myself – me and Jane together.
Or I was going to give it to my friend Luke Barker to buy me out and take
me on as his boy. Or else I was going to buy a big house and live by the
sea. I had all sorts of plans! Just to have it in my pocket made me feel
different, special – someone important. It was worth it just for that.

But in my heart I knew what was what. In the end Mother Shelly got to
hear I'd been hanging around the jewellers and wanted to know what I
was up to, so I gave her the ring, like I always knew I would.

Treasure isn't for rubbish kids, you see. It's too much. Really it just wastes
a kid's time. If you were sensible you'd chuck it away if you found some
treasure because it just spells trouble, but I don't think anyone could be
that sensible.

From Melvin Burgess, *The Baby and Fly Pie*

Activity 2 | Use an unreliable narrator

Authors often tell a story through a character whose account cannot entirely be trusted. This makes them interesting as a character, but it also makes us wonder about the 'truth' behind the story.

1 Read Extract A opposite. How reliable do you think the narrator is? On what evidence?
2 Write two separate first-person accounts of one incident by two narrators who were both present. Show their characters and viewpoints in their narratives.

Activity 3 | Write in the third person as an all-knowing narrator

Authors sometimes write from an all-knowing, or **omniscient**, viewpoint. This means they can tell the reader about any detail in the story, or any character's thoughts or feelings. Some authors even comment on the story, or address the reader directly.

1 Read Extract B opposite to see an example.
2 Rewrite the paragraphs you wrote in Activity 2 as a single paragraph. This time write in the third person as an omniscient narrator. You can now reveal what 'really' happened, and what your characters were thinking or feeling. You can even comment, or address the reader as 'you'.

Activity 4 | Write in the third person from one character's viewpoint

One effective way to write is in the third person but from one character's viewpoint. This means you can describe whatever action you like, but still encourage the reader to identify with one character – as if seeing things through that character's eyes.

1 Read Extract B opposite. See how it begins from the all-seeing narrator viewpoint, and comes back to it. But in the middle it slips into Millie's viewpoint, suggesting her thoughts.

2 Continue Extract B in your own way, imagining Millie's character and what happens. Choose **one** of these voices:
- write in the first person, as Millie
- write in the third person, but suggesting what Millie thinks and feels. For example, you could begin, 'The passage seemed very long. And what was that strange sound?' This would suggest that Millie is asking herself the question.

Extract A

Addresses us, assuming we think him mad

Repetition makes him sound excited, and pleased with himself

Now this is the point. You fancy me mad. Madmen know nothing. But you should have seen me. You should have seen how wisely I proceeded – with what caution – with what foresight – with what dissimulation I went to work! I was never kinder to the old man than during the whole week before I killed him. And every night, about midnight, I turned the latch of his door and opened it – oh so gently! And then, when I had made an opening sufficient for my head, I put in a dark lantern, all closed, closed, so that no light shone out, and then I thrust in my head. Oh, you would have laughed to see how cunningly I thrust it in! I moved it slowly – very, very slowly, so that I might not disturb the old man's sleep. It took me an hour to place my whole head within the opening so far that I could see him as he lay upon his bed. Ha! Would a madman have been so wise as this?

Anticipates our reaction

Challenges us, not wanting to be thought mad

Edgar Allan Poe, 'The Tell-Tale Heart'

Expand your vocabulary

dissimulation – clever concealment

Extract B

As if we are asking

What had happened to Millie?

Addresses us

All-knowing author's interpretation

She had left Sam's bedside, if you remember, after two ugly fights. The first she'd won handsomely. The second had humiliated her and she'd been thrown out into the corridor. She had sat for ten minutes or so, waiting for the throbbing in her head to die down. She calmed herself. Clearly, Sanchez was quick and well trained: some kind of martial artist, she imagined. Next time she would find an appropriate weapon.

Comforting herself with this thought, Millie stood up. It was dinnertime after all, and time to find again the bomb-site that the strange cook had called a dining hall. She descended the main staircase and set off along one of the school's many long, poorly-lit corridors.

Comments on situation

Everybody makes mistakes, particularly in new surroundings. Millie had never mastered her left and her right and she should have taken the first turning.

Andy Mulligan, *Ribblestrop*

1

Planning narrative and description

I am learning how to:

➜ decide the best way to plan my writing

➜ ensure my plans link with the paragraphs I need in my writing.

Activity 1 | Planning a narrative

A plan can help you decide the elements of a narrative and the order of events in your story. It is a very important part of creating your narrative.

First, you need to gather together your ideas on what might go into your story: for example, setting, character and plot. You can use a planning diagram to do this, such as a concept map or a tree diagram.

This student has used a spider diagram with headings for **characters**, **setting** and **events** in their story.

Events
– Leon finds pond – Brandon arrives
– threats – scuffles
– swimming – Leon good – under water contest – wins
– Brandon accepts loss
– back home – mother relieved

Characters
– main – Leon feeling alone after joining new school – seen as geeky – unpopular – good at swimming
– Brandon – king of the year group – strong – confident – knows his way around
– mother concerned about boy's unhappiness – doesn't want to interfere

Title – **Underwater**

Setting
– remote – woods – pond – hidden
– home – ends there
– school – boy remembers humiliation

It is a good idea to give each section a heading to help ensure you think of ideas for each of those categories. You could add extra sections, such as 'Atmosphere'.

Next, the student decided to take their ideas and plan the narrative in more detail using a sequencing diagram to show the order in which the story would be written.

This is a flexible way to plan adding extra events and features such as flashbacks.

1 Plan a story of your own, first, use a spider diagram to collect your initial ideas. Next, plan it is more detail using these headings:

Opening   **Dilemma**   **Conclusion**

Choose a title from the list below or use one of your own.
● The bargain   ● Snowstorm   ● Candyfloss

Activity 2 Planning a description

To plan a descriptive piece of writing, like planning a narrative, you also need to collect ideas and then decide the order in which to write them.

This student has used a diagram to collect ideas for a description of tennis player Laura Robson, listing ideas for the description next to each heading.

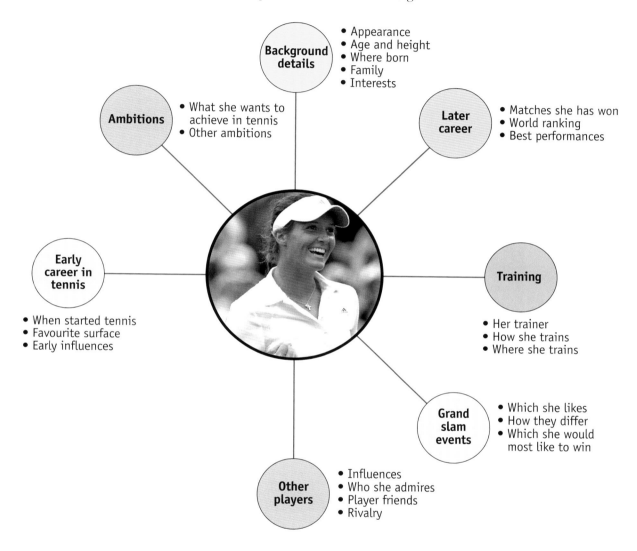

Background details
- Appearance
- Age and height
- Where born
- Family
- Interests

Ambitions
- What she wants to achieve in tennis
- Other ambitions

Later career
- Matches she has won
- World ranking
- Best performances

Early career in tennis
- When started tennis
- Favourite surface
- Early influences

Training
- Her trainer
- How she trains
- Where she trains

Grand slam events
- Which she likes
- How they differ
- Which she would most like to win

Other players
- Influences
- Who she admires
- Player friends
- Rivalry

The description could be ordered in different ways. Now the student needs to decide which order to use. In this plan, they could number each circle to show the order.

1 Look at the student's plan and use it to decide the order in which you would write this description of Laura Robson.

2 Now, plan your own description using a planning diagram to collect ideas.

Label and number each section on the planning diagram to show the order in which you are going to write.

2 Planning: explanation and argument

I am learning how to plan an explanation and an argument so that I can:

➜ decide the best way to plan my writing

➜ ensure my plans link with the paragraphs I need in my writing.

Your writing task

Write a detailed plan for an explanation or an argument:

1 Gather your ideas about the topic.
2 Decide the order for the points in your writing.
3 Plan the content for your introduction and conclusion.
4 Remember that each point on the plan will become a paragraph in the writing.
5 Write a first draft.
6 Review, revise and proofread.

Activity 1 | Planning an explanation

When planning an explanation, collect your ideas on a planning diagram, as for a narrative or description.

Look at this planning diagram that a student has used to collect ideas for an explanation of how to photograph the night sky.

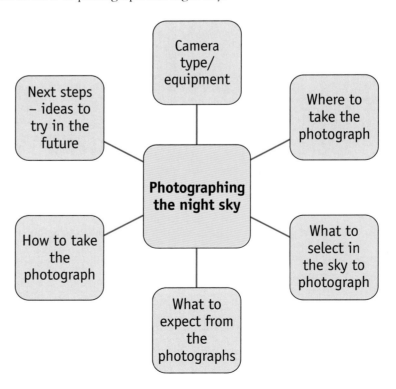

In an explanation, getting the key ideas in the right sequence is very important. You need to write the explanation in a logical order in order for readers to be able to follow it. The student used a flow diagram to organise the order of the sections of their explanation and to plan in more detail what would be included:

Photographing the night sky

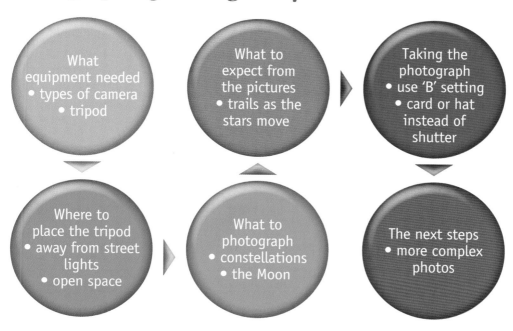

1 Organise these notes – explaining how to find a good gym and how to learn to train and keep safe – into a proper plan.

Activity 2 Planning an argument essay

When planning writing that is presenting an argument, think about the points in favour or against the topic. Plan what you are going to say in your introduction and conclusion.

There are two main ways of organising argument writing:

- Write about all the points in favour of the topic and then about all the points against. This is the most straightforward way of organising an argument but it can mean that those arguments that come in the second half of the essay have more influence because the reader comes to them last.
- The other way is to alternate a point in favour with a point against until you reach the conclusion. This can provide a more balanced essay because the arguments for and against are included alongside each other throughout.

1 Read these points for an argument essay about allowing 16-year-olds to vote.

Young people can join the army at 16 so should be able to vote.

Young people wouldn't take voting seriously.

Young people have too little experience of life to make a decision on voting.

16-year-olds can get married so should be responsible enough to vote.

Many 16-year-olds don't take an interest in politics so they would just vote as their parents told them.

Many important aspects of life affect 16-year-olds so they should have a say in what happens.

a) Decide whether each point is in favour or against allowing young people to vote and write it in the for or against column in a table like the one below.

b) Number each point in the order you would use for writing the argument.

c) Write the conclusion to the argument and explain what you think.

Lowering the voting age to 16	
Begin by writing an introduction.	
Points for being able to vote at 16	**Points against being able to vote at 16**
Finally, write your conclusion.	

Activity 3 | Plan and write an argument

1 Choose **one** of these topics:
- a discussion of the positive and negative aspects of mobile phones for young people

- a discussion of the points in favour and against young people having part-time jobs while they are studying.

2 Plan an argument essay on your chosen topic. Follow this order as you plan:
- a) Collect your ideas about the topic. You may need to do some initial research to find out more about the issue and the arguments that people use in favour or against.
- b) Remember to decide the order for the points in your writing and that each point on the plan will become a paragraph.
- c) Plan the content of your introduction and conclusion.
- d) Write a first draft of your argument.

Drafting, editing and proofreading

I am learning how to review my writing so that I can:

➡ check whether the writing makes good sense

➡ check whether parts need editing

➡ correct errors of spelling, punctuation, tense and agreement.

Your writing task

Review some writing of your own and improve its accuracy and effectiveness.

Activity 1 | Reviewing your writing

Reviewing your writing is an important task. As you read through your work you need to think about what you can improve. The improvements you can make include:

- checking for errors of punctuation, spelling and tense
- deciding whether the order of the writing is effective
- adding new sections if needed
- deleting sections that are less successful or irrelevant.

Whenever you are reviewing your work, it is important to check **spelling**. One of the trickiest things is to spot words that sound the same but are spelt differently, like 'their', 'there' and 'they're'.

Another thing to look out for when you are proofreading is **punctuation**.

1 Correct the spelling in this sentence.

> There mother was in four a suprise when thay get home and sore the fancy dress costumes they had highered for the party.

Make sure that your writing uses tense consistently and that the use of agreement is correct. For example, if a piece is written in the past tense, it should stay in that tense throughout.

2 Correct this extract by adding correct punctuation.

> Youll never guess who I saw down at the swimming pool said Lorna excitedly No who replied Tilly looking very interested

3 Correct the use of tense and agreement in this sentence:

> She is runs as fast as she can but the dog was gets away from her all the time.

Check whether your writing uses first, second or third **person** consistently.

4 Correct the use of first, second or third person in this sentence:

> He walks down towards the shops where I was going to meet my friends.

Activity 2   Practise reviewing writing

1 Review this short section from a draft piece of writing and identify what needs to be improved. Remember to focus on:

- the overall clarity and effectiveness of the piece
- spelling
- punctuation
- tense and person agreement
- parts that could be changed by cutting sections out, or rewriting them to improve them.

As he arrived at the sports centre, Josh is looking forward to seeing Ahmed as they hadn't met for a couple of weeks. Suddenly, he seed Ahmed by a table in the café but instead of the friendly greeting Josh expected, Ahmed just turned away and got on with talking to a crowd of people Josh hadn't seen before. Hey Ahmed called Josh but he just continued talking ignoring Josh completely. It was later in the changing rooms that things turnd ugly. So look who it is said Ahmed sniggering it's the geek. Yes he's a real geek from my school. The others laughed and began to surround the two. Well at least I don't forget my mates do I. The name-calling soon turned to pushes and shoves and finaly the first punch was thrown. As they are fighting, the crashed open and the athletics coach Sam Armitt burst in. Grabbing the two combatants by the arms he pulled them into the office and told them both that they were banned from the centre until both sets of parents had been called in. Josh wandered home wondering how he was going to explain the cuts and his torn shirt to his mum. later that evening Josh's phone beeped and there was a text from Ahmed beginning sorry mate, I was out of order.

Activity 3   Review your own writing

1 Review some recent extended writing of your own. This can be from any subject.

- Check for errors of spelling, punctuation and tense.
- Ensure the order of events described is effective.
- Add new sections to make it more successful.
- Remove sections that don't seem to work.

Know how to write texts that inform and explain

I am learning to improve my writing so that I can:

→ write about facts in a clear and helpful way

→ convey information that interests a target audience

→ explain ideas, and cause and effect.

Your writing task

Write an introductory information guide to the internet for people who do not know how it can be used.

Word count: around 150–200 words   **Number of paragraphs:** 3–4

Add annotations and commentary to features of your text showing how you present information and explain things effectively.

Activity 1 Write about information in a clear and logical way

Information texts present facts and ideas in a clear and logical way.

1 Read the information text opposite and see how it presents information clearly. Consider:

- its purpose
- how it is tailored to a particular audience
- how it progresses in a logical order from one point to the next.

2 Write your own paragraph for computer owners who have never used social media sites, telling readers what they offer. Plan your writing so that you can set out the information clearly and logically. Use headings if you wish.

3 Write your own paragraph for people who use social media but are unaware of the risks and how to avoid them. Use information from the text opposite, and whatever knowledge you have yourself of these risks and safeguards. In addition to the information in the text, you may want to include some of the following:

- writing Facebook updates or tweets that you later regret
- spending too much time on them
- being fooled into a relationship with people who want to exploit you

4 Re-read the paragraphs you have just written. Now combine the key points in a third paragraph weighing up the benefits and risks. You may find it useful to use some of the words and phrases below:

on the other hand   despite this   although   nonetheless   on the whole

Fake Facebook notification emails

These notifications will come to your email box and look like **legitimate** official Facebook emails, telling you that you have a new friend, someone posted a photo of you, or tagged you on a photo. You will want to click on the link in the email to see who has requested to be friends, or more **compelling**, who posted a photo of you. But once you click on that link, the trouble begins. The link may begin to install software on your computer, called spyware, which keeps track of your keystrokes, seeking out passwords to your accounts. Or clicking on the link may install 'worm' software and use your computer as a 'slave' computer – launching cyber attacks from your computer, all without you even knowing it. The link could download a virus that will render your computer useless. Or the link could redirect you to a webpage that will render your computer useless. Or the link could redirect you to a webpage that looks exactly like Facebook (but it will be **bogus**). Once redirected to a new webpage, you will likely be asked to log in again, thus collecting your Facebook login information. Now the scammer can go into your Facebook account and send spam to other users, spreading the scam even further.

Some of these emails are more scary in tone. They may say that a friend has reported

you to Facebook for a violation of their terms, instructing you to click on the link in order to review the report. Of course, any normal person is going to want to click on that link to see why they were reported. But it's a **scam**.

You may ask yourself, 'What do scammers get out of this?' They do not appear to get money out of this particular scam, but they also have a desperate need for other people's 'bandwidth' and account access, in order to send out hundreds of thousands of their emails or messages. Those messages may be targeting other people to steal their money. Scammers also need to send emails or messages out in stealth mode, in a way that cannot be traced back to them.

Social Media Scams, Kathleen McMahon

Annotations (left margin):

- Introductory sentence: possible versions listed
- Your likely response
- Technical terms used and explained
- Sentence announcing next section – consequences
- Straightforward, concise language
- Topic sentence for paragraph

Annotation (right margin):

- Raises question, then answers it

Expand your vocabulary

legitimate – genuine
compelling – attractive
bogus – false
scam – organised trick to obtain money

Activity 2 | Explain ideas

A text which **explains** usually presents some facts, but unlike a simple information text, it shows how they relate to each other. It is likely to do one of two things:

● enable the reader to understand an idea or concept

● present a process, showing a sequence of cause and effect.

1 Read Extract A opposite and see how it explains the concepts of weather and climate. Here are some of the things it does:

  ● brings the idea to life by relating it to what the reader knows or can easily see

  ● uses questions to explore the idea

  ● makes comparisons and uses 'signposting' phrases to indicate this

  ● uses examples

  ● explains technical terms

  ● sums up a point.

2 Imagine you have time-travelled to the Victorian era. Write an explanation of something from the twenty-first century for Victorian readers, using similar techniques to those in Extract A. For example, you could explain a computer, an aeroplane, or a phone.

Activity 3 | Explain cause and effect

1 Read Extract B opposite, which explains cause and effect. See how it does this. Notice how it makes connections and uses the word 'because'. What techniques does it have in common with Extract A?

2 Write three sentences explaining why you are (or are not) at school today, using the word 'because'.

consequently	for example	therefore	despite this	so
in addition	however	on the other hand	in comparison	in a similar way

3 a) Find some of these connectives in Extract A.

  b) Choose two or three of the connectives above and explain the job they do in a paragraph. Use examples to help you to explain.

Activity 4 | Write an introductory guide

1 Write an introductory guide to the internet for people who do not know how it can be used. Include:

  ● useful facts

  ● explanation of terms and ideas

  ● explanation of how the internet works in practice

  ● helpful subheadings.

2 Make sure you have presented the information in a logical order. Check that your subheadings actually describe what follows them. Annotate your text to show your uses of suitable language.

Extract A

Weather and climate

Relates to what reader knows

Uses questions

Signposts a comparison

Weather is what you see when you look out of your window. What do you see now – sunshine, rain, cloud, snow? Does it feel warm or cold? Does it look windy? All of this adds up to the weather. The weather can change in a day, or even an hour. Climate, on the other hand, is the pattern of weather over a long period of time, perhaps fifty, a hundred, or even a thousand years.

The world can be divided into different climate zones. We call the British type of climate 'temperate', meaning that it never becomes very hot or very cold, compared with other parts of the world. Similarly, if you look at average rainfall in Britain, it is neither very wet nor very dry. It may seem wet at times, but we never have torrential rainfall for days or weeks on end, as in the Indian monsoon. Climate, then, refers to averages over a long period of time.

Explains a term

Sums up

Extract B

Earth's climate is changing and people's activities are the main cause

The Earth is getting warmer because people are adding heat-trapping gases to the atmosphere, mainly by burning fossil fuels. These gases are called greenhouse gases. Warmer temperatures are causing other changes around the world, such as melting glaciers and stronger storms. These changes are happening because the Earth's air, water, and land are all linked to the climate. The Earth's climate has changed before, but this time is different. People are causing these changes, which are bigger and happening faster than any climate changes that modern society has ever seen before.

Know how to write summaries

I am learning to:

→ understand what is important in a text
→ select and order information
→ write information in my own words
→ combine sentences fluently and concisely.

Your writing task

Write a summary of an article. Start by finding out what a summary
is. Then practise the skills involved.
Word count: 90–100 words

Activity 1 — Understand what is important in a text

Texts often have to fit a limited space. A **summary** is a shortened version of a text
containing the most important information. To write one you need to understand the
text and decide what information is most important.

1 Read the passage opposite, from the website for *Rough Guide* travel guides.

The list below summarises the first paragraph in six bullet points. It captures the
main information and re-presents it so that these points are easily noted by the
reader. Notice that these bullet points are not all complete sentences.

- Turkey a mixture of exotic and familiar
- Combines influences from surrounding areas
- Has been invaded and settled throughout history
- Christians and Muslims coexist
- Range of ancient monuments
- Cultural traditions as popular as modern entertainment and sport.

2 a) Find the part of the text from which each point above is taken.
b) Make a similar bullet-point summary of the second paragraph.

Activity 2 — Select and order information

1 Sometimes you need to summarise information on one aspect of a text, and put it
in a logical order. List the points you can find in the text about Turkey's history.
2 Check to see if these points are in a logical order. If not, reorder them.

Turkey

With its **unique** mix of the exotic and the familiar, visiting Turkey can be a **mesmerising** experience. More than the 'bridge between East and West' of tourist-brochure **cliché**, the country combines influences from the Middle East and the Mediterranean, the Balkans and central Asia. Invaded and settled from every direction since the start of recorded history, its contradictions and fascinations persist. Mosques coexist with churches, Roman theatres and temples crumble not far from ancient Hittite cities, and **dervish** ceremonies or gypsy festivals are as much a part of the social landscape as classical music concerts or **avidly** attended football matches.

Another **facet** of Turkey that makes it such a rewarding place to travel is the Turkish people, whose reputation for friendliness and hospitality is richly deserved; indeed you risk causing offence by declining invitations and find yourself making friends through the simplest of **transactions**. Of course at the big resorts and tourist spots this can simply be [a way of] selling you something, but in most of the country the warmth and generosity is genuine – all the more amazing when much recent Turkish history saw outsiders mainly bringing trouble in their wake.

Politically modern Turkey was a grand experiment, largely the creation of one man – Kemal Atatürk. Endowed with **fervent** patriotism and superhuman energy, he salvaged the Turkish state from the wreckage of the Ottoman Empire and defined it as a modern, **secular** nation – his statue gazes down from public squares across the land. While the country's secular status remains intact for now, most of the inhabitants are at least nominally Muslim.

Rough Guide website

Expand your vocabulary

unique – there is nothing else like it
mesmerising – fascinating
cliché – tired, over-used phrase or idea
dervish – a religious group
avidly – keenly
facet – aspect
transactions – meetings or dealings with people
fervent – passionate
secular – having a non-religious government

Activity 3 · Present information in your own words

When summarising, it is best to present information in your own words. This will help you to use fewer words and to focus on the key points. A useful technique is to replace words with a single word or phrase, reordering sentences if necessary. For example:

> Turkish people like sport. For example, they like football. They also enjoy watching camels wrestling with each other. (Long)
>
> Turks enjoy sports such as football and camel wrestling. (Short)

1 Rewrite the following in fewer words by replacing the phrases in bold:
   a) I have **granola, muesli or cornflakes** for breakfast.
   b) Camel owners **make sure their camels are not hurt.**
   c) Camels are **made to look festive and appealing.**
   d) **Providing food for** a camel **and keeping it somewhere can cost a great deal of money.**

Activity 4 · Combine sentences fluently and concisely

1 Read the passage opposite, then the summary below of what its first paragraph tells us about camel wrestling.

> Camel wrestling has many fans, each village having its own prize Tulu fighting camel, some of which become famous. For fighting, they wear a decorated, straw-stuffed wooden frame over their hump and are hung with bells and shiny cloth.

Notice how the paragraph has been shortened:
- It has been reduced to two sentences by combining and reordering.
- Less important information has been omitted, such as:
  – Tulu being 'a special cross-breed'
  – the comparison with 'footballers or film stars' (we know what 'famous' means)
  – where the different bells were hung and their sound (we can guess).

2 Turn these sentences into a single, shorter one. Omit the reference to 'human wrestling'.

> A win is achieved by a camel either chasing his opponent away or causing him to overbalance. And, as in human wrestling, a fall can be caused by force or a simple trick.

Activity 5 · Write a summary

1 Summarise in 120–150 words what you learnt about camel wrestling in the passage opposite.

Camel wrestling in Turkey

Each village had its own prize camel, and each camel its own fan club, with many villagers travelling throughout the region to support it. These fighting camels were a special cross-breed, called Tulu. The famous ones were household names, and often as well known locally as footballers or film stars. For fighting, they carried, over their one hump, a *hauut*, a straw-stuffed wooden frame decorated with coloured rugs and with their names embroidered on the back. Bells hung off their necks and their backs, glittery material was draped along their bodies to adorn them, and each had a large brass bell under its chin which made a solid clang as they walked.

These festivals, organised by a local committee, all follow a similar formula. Each participating camel is paired with one similar in size, weight and championship record and another **crucial** aspect, one I would never have guessed at: just like humans, a camel is right-footed, left-footed and occasionally **ambidextrous**. So, it's necessary to pair up like with like – the wrong pairing would be like a left-footed person trying to dance the tango with a right-footed one – as you can't really teach a camel to use the other leg.

The festivals all begin with the smallest camels, the animals getting progressively bigger with each fight, and the day ending with the real heavyweights. The larger animals are also the most famous and by the time they're on, the crowd is at its biggest and most excitable. … The rules are quite straightforward: a win is achieved by a camel either chasing his opponent away or causing him to overbalance. And, as in human wrestling, a fall can be caused by force or a simple trick. Although it sounds as though **pitting** against each other two animals weighing several hundred kilos each would end in injury, the sport is not dangerous at all. In fact, the Turks consider this a **humanitarian** sport. They have great respect for the camel, and wouldn't allow anything which would cause it harm.

A Game of Polo with a Headless Goat, Emma Levine

Expand your vocabulary

crucial – very important
ambidextrous – able to use left or right hands or feet
pitting – fighting, one against another
humanitarian – concerned for the welfare of the participants

Know how to write instructional texts

I am learning to write instructional texts so that I can:

→ write clearly and concisely for a target audience

→ use precise language

→ break up information into well-ordered steps

→ combine text and pictures.

Activity 1 — Write clearly and concisely for a target audience

To write instructions, use **imperatives** – verbs that tell readers to do something. For example:

| put | twist | take | spread | click | pour | stir |

1 Write four short instructional sentences using four of these verbs.

Sometimes it helps to add an **adverb**, before or after the verb, explaining **how** a reader should do something, like this:

Spread the icing **evenly**.

2 Extend the meaning of two of your sentences by including adverbs.

Instructions should take into account:

● what the reader will not know or need to have explained
● what they may get wrong or find confusing
● anything that should happen at a particular stage
● what order is most helpful.

3 Read Extract A and identify how Dan could improve the directions that he has emailed to his French penpal on how to find his house.

4 Rewrite Dan's directions so that Thierry will be able to follow them.
● Make up any necessary details not included.
● Leave out unnecessary details.
● Keep the directions to the same length or shorter.

Extract A

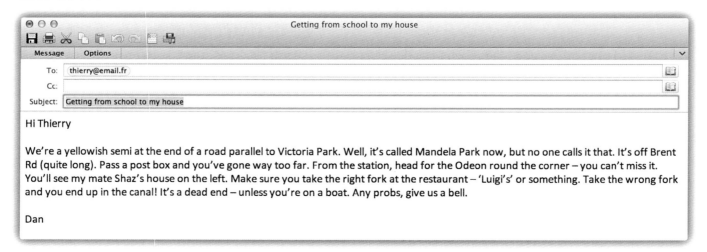

Subject: Getting from school to my house

To: thierry@email.fr

Subject: Getting from school to my house

Hi Thierry

We're a yellowish semi at the end of a road parallel to Victoria Park. Well, it's called Mandela Park now, but no one calls it that. It's off Brent Rd (quite long). Pass a post box and you've gone way too far. From the station, head for the Odeon round the corner – you can't miss it. You'll see my mate Shaz's house on the left. Make sure you take the right fork at the restaurant – 'Luigi's' or something. Take the wrong fork and you end up in the canal! It's a dead end – unless you're on a boat. Any probs, give us a bell.

Dan

Activity 2 Use precise language

Remember to write instructions in a fairly formal way unless they are for a friend. Choose words precisely, especially nouns and verbs, to avoid confusion. Using a formal word or technical term may be more concise. Extracts B and C are two examples of effective instructions.

Extract B

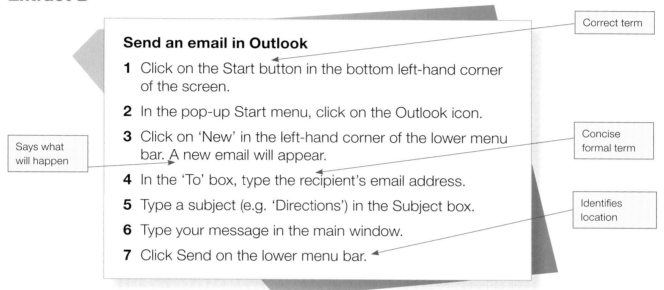

Send an email in Outlook

1 Click on the Start button in the bottom left-hand corner of the screen.

2 In the pop-up Start menu, click on the Outlook icon.

3 Click on 'New' in the left-hand corner of the lower menu bar. A new email will appear.

4 In the 'To' box, type the recipient's email address.

5 Type a subject (e.g. 'Directions') in the Subject box.

6 Type your message in the main window.

7 Click Send on the lower menu bar.

Correct term

Says what will happen

Concise formal term

Identifies location

Extract C

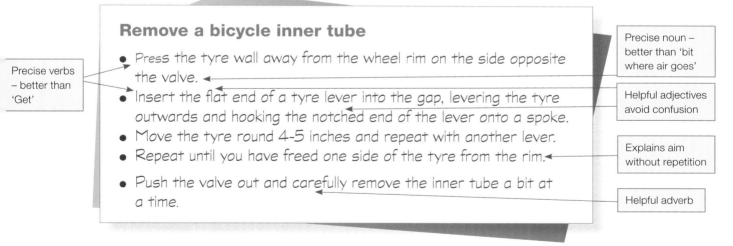

Remove a bicycle inner tube

● Press the tyre wall away from the wheel rim on the side opposite the valve.

● Insert the flat end of a tyre lever into the gap, levering the tyre outwards and hooking the notched end of the lever onto a spoke.

● Move the tyre round 4-5 inches and repeat with another lever.

● Repeat until you have freed one side of the tyre from the rim.

● Push the valve out and carefully remove the inner tube a bit at a time.

Precise verbs – better than 'Get'

Precise noun – better than 'bit where air goes'

Helpful adjectives avoid confusion

Explains aim without repetition

Helpful adverb

1 Write instructions for one of the following:

● making a simple meal of your choice

● getting from school to your home

● using your school's lunch system.

Activity 3 — Break up information into well-ordered steps

Instructions often need to be followed in an exact order. For example, you have to cook a cake before icing it! If you are writing instructions in a paragraph, use 'signposting' words and phrases to indicate order, such as:

> then   when   after   once   as soon as   now   after   while

1 a) Find the 'signposting' words and phrases in the following paragraph:

> Sit comfortably on the saddle, holding both handlebars, with one foot on the ground and one on a pedal. Now lean forward and press down hard on the pedal while balancing the bike. At the same time, place your other foot on the pedal and start pedalling. When you come to a corner, lean in towards it while steering gently round it. As you complete the turn, return to an upright position and straighten the handlebars.

b) How many separate steps are given here?

2 Write a short paragraph explaining how to do one of the following:
- take a penalty in football
- paint a wall
- write a story.

Readers may find it easier to follow a numbered or bullet-point list. The instructions opposite show how this can be done.

3 Read these instructions and find two each of the following:
- imperative verbs
- other precise verbs
- precise nouns
- helpful adjectives or adverbs.

Activity 4 — Combine text and pictures

1 Look at the labelled picture of a dome tent opposite. How does it help the reader when combined with the instructions?

2 How would you label the bike here to help someone following the instructions in Activity 3 (Exercise 1)?

Putting up a simple dome tent

You should have:

- inner tent
- flysheet with guy ropes attached
- tent poles in elastic-linked sections
- tent pegs.

Inner tent

1 Spread the tent out on flat ground with the door facing away from the wind.

2 Fix the sections of each tent pole together to form full-length poles. Lay these on the ground.

3 Feed each pole through one of the sleeves diagonally crossing the top of the tent.

4 Connect one end of each pole to its tent corner by inserting its end-piece into the metal ring at the corner.

5 Connect the poles to the last two corners to raise the tent into a dome. At this point you should be able to lift the tent and reposition it if necessary.

6 Peg each tent corner to the ground, using a mallet to drive in pegs through the loop at the corner of the tent. Insert the peg so that it leans slightly away from the tent and holds the corner to the ground. Tip: leave the tip of the peg above ground so you can remove it easily when you take the tent down.

Flysheet

1 Spread the flysheet over the inner tent, with its front over the tent door.

2 Tie the centre of the flysheet to the crossed centre of the tent poles.

3 Pull the flysheet's guy ropes outward and stake them to the ground. Adjust their length so that the flysheet is not touching the inner tent. Warning: very long guy ropes are easier to trip over!

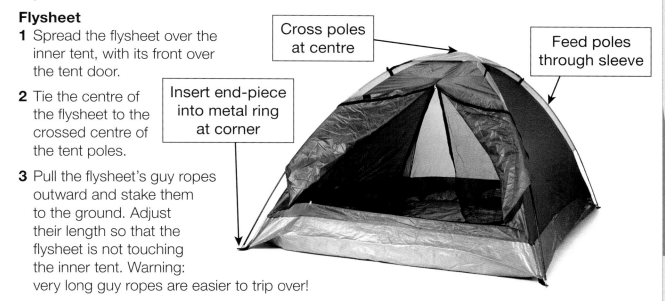

Cross poles at centre

Feed poles through sleeve

Insert end-piece into metal ring at corner

Activity 5 | Writing your own instructions

1 Think of something that you know how to do. Write instructions suitable for someone in your class who does not know how to do this.

- Write your instructions in the form that you think will work best.
- Add one or more labelled diagrams or pictures.
- Make sure your instructions are well ordered, clear and concise.

Know how to write texts that guide or advise

I am learning to write texts that guide or advise so that I can:
➜ use formal and informal language appropriately
➜ structure the advice helpfully
➜ engage with the reader
➜ consider the reader's options.

Activity 1 Write using an appropriate level of formality

Advice writing includes:
● health and safety leaflets
● 'agony aunt/uncle' columns
● guides to choosing a product.

Whatever the exact purpose, the language should be fairly formal, so that the reader takes you seriously. However, you also need to avoid putting the reader off, so a little humour may be effective at times.

1 Rewrite the following in more formal language.
   a) If you're stupid enough to swim in the sea where there's no lifeguard, you deserve to die a horrible death by drowning.
   b) If you look like a three-year-old attacked you with a red felt tip, you think you're gonna throw up, and you feel like you're on fire – dude, you've got chickenpox!
   c) So you're 14 and you're, like, 'Poor me, no one understands me, boo hoo.' Well, surprise, surprise: you're not the first. Just get a grip and get over yourself!

Activity 2 Structure the advice helpfully

If you give advice to the public, break it into sections and arrange these in a logical order.

1 Read the Royal National Lifeboat Institution advice opposite and see how it is broken down, as well as being written with an appropriate level of formality.

   It may help to use headings. Even if you don't, it is a good test of structure to see if each of your sections could be given a single heading.

2 Write the text for a page of a leaflet on 'Avoiding difficulties' in one of the following situations:
   ● at school
   ● online
   ● on the sports field
   ● on the street.

   Structure your advice helpfully and use an appropriate level of formality.

Beach safety advice

There's nothing better than hitting the beach on a sunny day. But don't let your day be ruined by trouble in the water.

With more people visiting the beach than ever before, our lifeguards and lifeboat crews have never been busier. We believe that, by providing beach safety advice and education programmes, many more lives can be saved.

- Wherever possible, swim at a lifeguarded beach. Go to www.goodbeachguide.co.uk to search for listings throughout the UK, or find a lifeguarded beach in the Republic of Ireland on the Irish Water Safety website.
- Always read and obey the safety signs, usually found at the entrance to the beach. These will help you avoid potential hazards on the beach and identify the safest areas for swimming.
- When on a lifeguarded beach, find the red and yellow flags and always swim or bodyboard between them – this area is patrolled by lifeguards.
- Never swim alone.
- If you get into trouble, stick your hand in the air and shout for help.
- If you see someone in difficulty, don't attempt a rescue. Tell a lifeguard, or, if you can't see a lifeguard, call 999 or 112 and ask for the coastguard.
- If you are hiring equipment for a surfsport, try to do so from a member of the Surf Hire Safety Scheme. Scheme members check equipment regularly for damage, rent out equipment suitable to your ability and offer safety advice for the local area. Read more or find an outlet.

Addresses reader in second person

Friendly start avoids putting reader off

Logical order, from basic to 'what if'

Clear imperatives

Slightly informal to be direct

Activity 3 | Engage with the reader

In advice writing, it is usually better to address the reader using the second-person pronoun **you**:

> Only swim where you know it's safe.

For some types of advice it is also helpful to acknowledge the reader as an individual:

> If you're the kind of person who gets nervous, try taking slow, deep breaths.

1 Rewrite the following to engage the reader:
   a) Getting lost in the woods is dangerous. Those who do not know them well should carry a map and compass.
   b) If hiking in winter, several layers of warm clothing should be worn.
   c) Care should be taken at all times near the cliff edge. In addition it is a good idea to carry a mobile phone.
2 a) Advice should move from sympathetic understanding to solutions. Read the 'agony uncle' advice opposite and notice how it does this.
   b) Imagine that Martians have begun to live on Earth. Write a helpful reply to a letter from a 14-year-old Martian in your school who is being teased about being different.

Activity 4 | Consider the reader's options

The agony uncle opposite considers the letter-writer's options, then recommends one. Sometimes the adviser may have to leave a final decision to the reader.

1 If you are advising on buying a product, you can use some 'signposting' phrases:

> on the other hand   in addition   by comparison   however   despite this

Choose three of these and for each write two sentences of advice on buying a product of your choice using the phrase to start the second sentence, followed by a comma. For example:

> You'll be able to run more apps on an iPhone than on the HTC Wildfire. On the other hand, the Wildfire is a quarter of the price.

2 Add to one of your sentence pairs to write a paragraph of advice comparing two or more products.

Activity 5 | Survive on a desert island

1 Use all that you now know to write a page of helpful, well-structured and encouraging advice for a group of school students shipwrecked without adults on a desert island.

Dear Agony Uncle Dave

My mother died years ago and my father worries about me all the time. He won't even let me visit my granny in case I get into trouble in the woods on the way. I really want to go and see her, and anyway, she's a sick old lady and I'd like to take her a few goodies.

My dad is a woodcutter, so he's out all day. I just don't know if I should tell him how much it means to me to see my granny, or just go and hope he doesn't find out. His attitude is really getting to me. What should I do?

RRH

Immediate sympathy

Dear RRH

I understand how you feel. You must miss your mother, even if she died some time ago, and your father probably misses her terribly, even if he doesn't talk about it. (Woodcutters tend to be strong, silent types!) Try to understand that he isn't just trying to restrict you. He loves you and is probably worried that he will lose you too. Also, as a woodcutter, he knows what kind of dangers there are in the woods, so don't ignore his warnings.

You could tell your father how much you want to go, but if he still says no, then it would seem even worse to disobey him. Perhaps it is best to avoid a confrontation. Visit your granny, and take her a basket of goodies, but make sure you stick to the path. Don't go picking primroses till you're lost in the woods. If you meet any strangers, don't get drawn into conversation - and don't mention where you're going. This especially applies to wolves, and even more so to big bad ones. If pressed on this, say you're going to the zoo - that's the last place a wolf will want to go!

Shows understanding

Points out father's side in reassuring way

Sensible

Explores options

Solution

Sensible warning ('don't')

Ends on light note

Know how to write texts that argue or debate

I am learning to improve my writing techniques so that I can:

→ build my argument point by point
→ get my argument in first
→ use opening and closing killer sentences
→ repeat and chain together my key words and phrases.

Your writing task

Write an argument for or against reintroducing into Britain the animals that once lived here, like wolves and bears.
Word count: around 200–250 words
Add annotations to label your uses of language and how they are effective.

To improve your own writing, in this section and the next section you are going to investigate writing techniques used in arguments.

Activity 1 Build your argument point by point

1 To start with, what do you think about the argument yourself? List three reasons for and three against zoos. Use convincing points and persuasive language, for example:

> **For:** It enriches our education to see swinging monkeys, exotic reptiles, growling tigers …
>
> **Against:** Zoos are prisons where innocent creatures are unjustly held captive.

2 Now read an expert's argument for zoos in Extract A, opposite. This extract was written for a magazine and the writers had up to 350 words to make their points quickly and powerfully. Notice that the writer makes a number of key points. He builds them up idea by idea so they are in a logical order. This means the reader can easily follow his flow of argument.

3 Match each key point of the argument listed below to the correct paragraph, to put the writer's argument in the correct order. Notice how each key point is developed in its own paragraph. This is important in helping the reader to follow the flow of ideas.

    a) Zoos keep endangered animals safe and well.
    b) Those who wish to see zoos banned don't know enough about the good that zoos do, and want to stop people having pleasure and learning about animals.
    c) If we didn't have zoos, endangered species would die out as they can't easily be returned to the wild.
    d) Zoos support conservation in the wild because they are places where animals can be studied.
    e) Young people learn lots from direct contact with animals in zoos.

Extract A

Do we need zoos?

Yes

The strongest argument for keeping zoos is based on education and inspiration: 100 000 children come to London Zoo each year to be taught about animals. Films of wild animals on television are wonderful but they give little sense of scale or of what a living animal is like to smell or touch (when this is allowed). Importantly, people who come to zoos learn about conservation and many are motivated to do something about preserving animal life.

The Zoological Society of London runs more than 100 conservation projects in the wild. These are nourished by scientific understanding derived from studies of captive animals. People in countries where animals are threatened learn about building capacities for conservation and acquire veterinary training and techniques for managing small populations. In turn, zoos benefit from what is learnt by the field workers.

Providing high standards of care is crucial in a well-run zoo and is required by law. Knowledge of how to measure the welfare of animals has driven great improvements in the ways animals are kept. Enrichment and the use of modern techniques of reward, along with advances in nutritional science and veterinary care, have had enormous benefits.

Zoos are reservoirs for endangered species. Returning animals to the wild is challenging because captive-bred animals do not have the skills for finding food or evading predators. It requires great care and patience. If zoos were banned, would

their inhabitants be released into their natural habitats, to die from starvation?

Keeping animals in captivity is more complex and interesting than those who wish to ban zoos believe. Captivity must be weighed against the wider benefits of conservation. It is far from obvious that the sensitivities of the few, often prejudiced and ill informed, should deny pleasure and educational benefit to the millions who come to our excellent British zoos.

Patrick Bateson, President of the Zoological Society of London

Key term

Counter argument: this is the opposite view – 'counter' here means 'against' or 'opposing'

Activity 2   Get your argument in first

Notice that for each key point in the argument **for** zoos in Extract A, the writer thinks about what might be written **against** zoos – the counter argument. He writes his points in a way that shows the counter argument is wrong. This is a clever technique that good writers often use to get their argument in first.

1 For each point **for** zoos in the table, what might the writer have thought the argument **against** zoos might say – what counter argument has he anticipated?

Writer's key point	Counter argument the writer anticipates
Young people learn lots from direct contact with animals in zoos (paragraph 1)	Why do we need zoos now we have technology that shows animals where they should be, in the wild?
Zoos keep endangered animals safe and well (paragraphs 3-4)	
If we didn't have zoos, endangered species would die out as they can't easily be returned to the wild (paragraph 4)	

Activity 3   Use opening and closing killer sentences

Notice that the writer starts with his strongest argument – and tells you so:

> The strongest argument for keeping zoos is based on education and inspiration: 100 000 children come to London Zoo each year to be taught about animals.

Notice how he ends his argument:

> It is far from obvious that the sensitivities of the few, often prejudiced and ill informed, should deny pleasure and educational benefit to the millions who come to our excellent British zoos.

He cleverly returns to his main argument, the one he started with.

1 Look again at the last sentence of the argument.
   a) Who is the writer attacking?
   b) What does he want the reader to think about those who oppose zoos?
   c) What is the impact of the last four words: 'our excellent British zoos'?

Activity 4   Repeat and chain together key words and phrases

Notice that the writer of Extract A wants the reader to know how zoos are well run and managed with care, as well as their benefit to animals in the wild. To do this he uses words and phrases that are connected. They build an impression in the reader. You may not notice it happening, but as you follow the logic of the argument you are influenced by the choice of words.

1 Look again at the argument **for** zoos in Extract A. Explore how the writer's choice of words and phrases work behind the scenes on the mind of the reader.

- How many times is the word 'conservation' used?
- Which words and phrases link to the idea that zoos are run on scientific and welfare principles, for example, 'modern techniques'?
- Find the adjectives the writer has chosen to convince the reader that all is 'good' in zoos: for example, '**high** standards'.

Activity 5 Select facts

In argumentative writing, the writer chooses which facts to present.

1 Look at some of the pro-zoo writer's facts:

- 100 000 children come to London Zoo each year to be taught about animals.
- You cannot smell or touch animals on TV.
- The Zoological Society of London runs over 100 conservation projects in the wild.
- Standards of care in British zoos are enforced by law.

a) What kinds of facts are left out? Think of three facts or types of information that you could research. For example, how much space do tigers have in a zoo, and in the wild?

b) What questions would you ask about the facts in Extract A to test how valid they are? For example, do the children really come 'to be taught about animals', or just to see them?

Activity 6 Write your own argument

1 Some people want to reintroduce animals to Britain that have become extinct here. Possible species are the wolf, beaver, brown bear, and lynx. Some arguments **for** this are:

- They belong here and are only extinct because of human activity.
- They would be happier than in zoos and could be studied in the wild.
- They could be a useful part of the ecosystem; for example, wolves would keep deer numbers down.
- It would encourage tourism in areas like the Scottish Highlands.

Discuss the arguments **against** this idea. Then decide on which side you wish to argue.

2 Plan and write an argument for your case in 200–250 words.

Know how to write texts that persuade

9

I am learning how to:

→ drive my point of view home with impact and persuasive force
→ balance my sentences in two parts
→ use formal vocabulary – words and phrases to convince the reader I am an expert
→ select simple sentences for high impact.

Your writing task

Write a persuasive argument criticising a group of people (e.g. those who are for or against hunting).
Word count: around 200–250 words
Add annotations to label your uses of language and how they are effective.

Activity 1 — Reading as a writer

1 Read the argument against zoos in Extract B opposite. The writer has used special techniques in his argument such as:

- opening and closing killer sentences
- get your argument in first
- repeat and chain together key words and phrases.

Some of these have been highlighted. How many other examples can you find?

2 How has the writer constructed his argument point by point in a logical way?

Note down a short summary of the key points for each of the five paragraphs. For example:

> **Paragraph 1: Zoos don't help conservation because they focus on showing animals that attract visitors rather than preserving those at risk, and there isn't much evidence to show that going to a zoo helps to inform the public.**

Activity 2 — Balance a sentence using different viewpoints

Notice how the writer uses a sentence with two main ideas and the connective **but** to separate two views. For example:

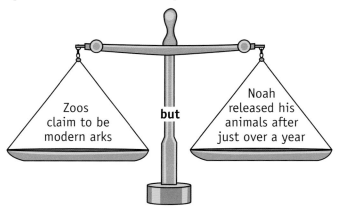

This helps him to get his argument across. The second part of the sentence 'counterbalances' the first part. It is an alternative viewpoint. It has more force as it ends the sentence. It is the view the writer wants you to share.

1 Find two more examples where the writer uses this technique.

Activity 3 Balance a sentence using a main idea and an explanation

Now notice how the writer uses a sentence with the main idea in the first part and the second part explaining or expanding it. A colon (:) separates the two parts of the sentence:

> Zoos are an anachronism: they were designed in the nineteenth century, to put animals on display so that people could see what they looked like.

The colon acts as a signal to the reader that more information is coming. It also makes the first part of the sentence more powerful as a statement in its own right. It gives it strength.

1 The colon could be replaced by a connective. Which one could you use? Would it work equally well?

Extract B

Do we need zoos?

No

Opening sentence challenges the main opposing view: that zoos help with conservation

There is no question that we need to meet the challenges posed in conserving biodiversity, but there is little evidence that zoos could ever help to meet these challenges. There is a great deal of information available on the conservation crisis that we are facing but there is little evidence that looking at animals in captivity helps the public to understand conservation issues or animal behaviour — not least because many zoos focus on charismatic species that attract visitors, not species at risk of extinction.

The writer anticipates the opposing argument and starts the paragraph by countering it

Most endangered vertebrates are not kept in zoos. Much better educational information is available on the web and in television programmes that focus on endangered species and more importantly, ecosystems.

Notice the chain of words and phrases linked to the idea that zoos are cruel places: 'welfare problems', 'small cages', 'confined areas', 'stressed animals', 'public display'

Zoos claim to be modern arks but Noah released his animals after just over a year. Zoos keep animals long term and such animals become unsuitable for release, in no small part owing to the considerable welfare problems that are associated with keeping wild animals in small cages or confined areas. Stressed animals

showing stereotypic behaviour cannot cope with life in the wild. Most successful reintroduction programmes have used animals held in short-term dedicated breeding facilities near the release site, not on public display in a zoo in another part of the world.

Zoos are an anachronism: they were designed in the nineteenth century, to put animals on display so that people could see what they looked like. In a changing world, zoos have tried to reinvent themselves as bodies devoted to education and conservation. In reality they are animal theme parks, with an ever-increasing number introducing rides and other entertainments in order to stay solvent.

The impending biodiversity crisis needs twenty-first-century solutions. Zoos are a very expensive distraction, not a solution.

Stephen Harris, Professor of Environmental Sciences

Activity 4 — Use formal vocabulary to show you are an expert

Notice how the writer of Extract B sprinkles his argument with scientific and academic words and phrases to strengthen his argument, such as:

conserving biodiversity
ecosystems

charismatic species
endangered vertebrates

1 Find another two examples where the writer has carefully chosen the vocabulary he uses for effect and wants you to believe he has superior knowledge.

Activity 5 — Use simple sentences for high impact

Notice how the writer of Extract B uses different kinds of sentences to achieve different outcomes. Many sentences are complex, for example, this detailed sentence.

> Zoos keep animals long term and such animals become unsuitable for release, in no small part owing to the considerable welfare problems that are associated with keeping wild animals in small cages or confined areas.

At other times the writer wants to make one big point really clearly and chooses a simple sentence to express his complete thought or idea. For example:

Stressed animals showing stereotypic behaviour cannot cope with life in the wild.

1 Below are two more examples where the writer chose to use simple sentences.

Notice where they occur in the text. How are they used? What impact do they have on you as a reader?

Most endangered vertebrates are not kept in zoos.

The impending biodiversity crisis needs twenty-first-century solutions.

Activity 6 — Use contrasting ideas to make a point

The writer of Extract B anticipates and dismisses a counter argument by using a sentence contrasting a positive idea and a negative one associated with zoos:

> Most successful reintroduction programmes have used animals held in short-term dedicated breeding facilities near the release site, not on public display in a zoo in another part of the world.

1 a) What is positive about the first idea here?
  b) What is negative about the second idea here?
2 Use the same technique of contrast within one sentence to write a sentence that first says what tigers should ideally be doing, in the wild, then gives a negative view of how they live in zoos.

Activity 7   Make a three-part statement

Persuasive writing needs a powerful conclusion to gather together the points it has made and drive them home without just repeating them. Notice how the anti-zoo writer begins his second-to-last paragraph with a short, sharp statement that sets its topic:

> Zoos are an anachronism: ….

By 'anachronism', the writer means that zoos are old-fashioned institutions invented in a time before we knew better and when people just wanted to see what exotic animals from other countries looked like.

The next sentence is about the zoos' efforts to survive:

> In a changing world, zoos have tried to reinvent themselves as bodies devoted to education and conservation.

1 a) Which word here is a clue that the writer does not think they have not succeeded in doing this?
   b) What phrase sums up the positive image that zoos have aimed to achieve?

The third sentence drives home the punch of the paragraph. The phrase 'In reality' signals that we are about to hear a negative truth about zoos to counter the positive idea in the previous sentence.

2 Now write your own paragraph using this same three-part formula:
   ● a statement criticising an institution or group of people (for example, supporters of hunting, or those against hunting)
   ● a statement about how that institution or group wants to be seen
   ● a statement beginning 'In reality' contradicting this view.

Activity 8   Drive home your points with a strong conclusion

1 The short concluding paragraph of Extract B reminds us of the urgent problem of biodiversity, and the need for 'solutions'. According to the final sentence, how do zoos make this problem worse?
2 Add a final paragraph on these lines to the paragraph you wrote for Activity 7. You need to spell out a problem, and explain how the person or group you are criticising only makes it worse.

Know how to write expository and narrative essays

Your writing tasks

1 Write a short expository essay about a famous person.

   Word count: around 150–200 words

2 Write an narrative essay about an experience that was difficult or dangerous for you.

   Word count: around 200–300 words

Learn techniques for this kind of writing. Then try them out. Add annotations to label some of your use of techniques and comment on them.

Key term

Essay: piece of writing which is usually written from the author's personal point of view. In an **expository** essay, you **expose** your ideas and feelings and explain them interestingly. A **narrative** essay tells a true story, for example, an account of an experience.

I am learning how to write essays so that I can:

→ explain my feelings

→ explain background

→ engage the reader's interest

→ tell a true story effectively.

Activity 1 Explain my feelings

1 A typical subject might be: 'A famous person who has inspired you'.
   a) Consider what famous person you could write about.
   b) Make a plan of points you could include, or which you would need to research.

2 Read the article opposite. The opening paragraph introduces sprinter Usain Bolt. It focuses on Bolt's name and achievement, using a superlative: 'fastest man on planet Earth'.
   a) How does this word choice sound impressive?
   b) Write a similar opening about someone you admire.

3 The next two sentences of the article compare Bolt's fame before and after 2008.
   a) What three facts do they cleverly include?
   b) Add two 'before and after' sentences to your own account, including two or three facts.

Activity 2 Explain background

1 Paragraph 2 of the article explains how Bolt's background helps to make him a hero, briefly telling his life story.
   a) How is Bolt's background significant?
   b) How does the writer use a list to show Bolt's importance?

2 Add a paragraph to your own account.
   a) Describe your hero's background.
   b) Use a list to show how he or she is significant to different sorts of people.

3 Paragraph 3 explains Bolt's national importance. The topic sentence begins:

   In an island riven by gang warfare and poverty …

   This shows why Jamaica needs a hero. The rest of the sentence describes Bolt's positive effect.

   Write a two-part sentence like this about your hero.

My hero: Usain Bolt

Guardian, 27 July 2012, by
Ian Thomson

Positive rhetorical question

States his achievement

Before and after

Interesting details

Was ever a sprint champion better named? Lightning bolt. Usain St Leo Bolt: the fastest man on planet Earth. Before he triumphed with a gold medal in 2008, only track diehards had heard of him. Now the 25-year-old Jamaican is famous worldwide. In spite of his fame he remains heroically down to earth and relaxed. He loves reggae and 'lyrically active' (verbally inventive) Jamaican dancehall DJs. He stands at 6 ft 5 in. He has survived a car crash. Yet he will not consider himself a legend unless he rules in London next week, as he did in Beijing four years ago.

Critics warn that e-cigarettes risk glamorising smoking among the young and could act as a gateway to the real thing. This is as laughable an argument as the idea that brightly coloured cigarette packaging 'encourages' children to start smoking. Both arguments are utter rubbish, of course.

From poverty to fame

Jamaica loves a hero, and no Jamaican is more heroic than Bolt. Born in 1986 on the island's rural north coast, he grew up poor. His parents ran a grocery store selling bottles of rum and cigarettes. By the age of 12, Bolt was the school's fastest 100 m sprinter; now he is a three-time Olympic gold medallist. All kinds of Jamaicans will be rooting for him next week at the starting blocks. Black, white, brown and yellow; **vested interests**, professionals, businesspeople; all will be joined in

optimism about their sporting hero and Jamaica's own future.

List

In an island **riven** by gang warfare and poverty, Bolt will help to rally Jamaicans to the black, gold and green of the national flag. As every Jamaican knows, the green is symbolic of hoped-for rebirth and the black a recognition of continental Africa. For years, Jamaica's African slave heritage was the dark area of self-denial in the national psyche. (To a degree, it still is.) Bolt gives an immense sense of pride not only to Jamaicans living in Jamaica, but to **diaspora** Jamaicans in the United States and the UK. This August, as Jamaica prepares to celebrate 50 years of independence from Britain, Usain Bolt will be a reason to jump (even sprint) for joy.

National significance

Looks to future on positive note

Expand your vocabulary

vested interests – people who will benefit if he wins
riven – divided
diaspora – people who have emigrated

Activity 3 | Engage the reader's interest

A **narrative** essay tells a true story, but how you present it is up to you. You could emphasise or leave out some details, or use flashback to tell the story in a new order.

Readers will be interested in many of the same things as in a fictional story:

- what is going to happen
- the character and feelings of the narrator (you)
- what the experience was like
- descriptive language.

1 Read the passage opposite, in which solo yachtswoman Ellen MacArthur describes steering her boat *Kingfisher* through seas littered with huge icebergs and 'growlers' (smaller ones). Find examples of how she interests us in the ways listed above.

2 Focus on the first paragraph.

  a) How does MacArthur make us understand the danger she was in?

  b) How does she reveal how she felt?

  c) How does she appeal directly to us?

Activity 4 | Tell a true story effectively

To tell a true story effectively, you have to make readers imagine the experience by using vivid language.

1 Focus on the second paragraph opposite.

  a) How does MacArthur make us realise how big the icebergs were?

  b) How does she appeal to our senses?

  c) How does she use vivid adjectives to suggest her possible fate?

2 How does MacArthur use descriptive language vividly in the final sentence of the extract?

Activity 5 | Combining narrative and explanation

1 Your task is to combine narrative and explanation by telling the story of an experience that was difficult or dangerous for you in some way. Use some of Ellen MacArthur's techniques to bring it to life.

  You must:

  - explain the context – for example, a sports event or a school test
  - tell the story dramatically, so that the reader understands what was at stake
  - explain what was difficult and how you felt
  - make the reader want to know what happened.

Sailing in the South Polar Seas

As morning broke I spotted the first berg looming out of the greyness of the sea and sky. I was in a state of expectant nervousness, laced with a thrill from the potential danger. You know that more than ever you are living on the edge, that you cannot fall asleep, and that profound dread of a splitting, crunching, gut-wrenching halt to your journey is ever present. You try not to think about the 'what ifs' of a collision with an iceberg weighing thousands of tons; you mustn't imagine how *Kingfisher* would react to an impact at **15 knots** with a cliff of solid ice any more than you would think of a car crash each time you went for a drive. …

There seemed no easy way through as although there were gaps between the bergs they were strewn with growlers, often still the size of cars or even houses. Most of the larger bergs looked like sections taken from the cliffs of Dover, hundreds of feet high and jagged with **crevasses**. Even sheltered from the icy wind outside, the cabin felt like a freezer. …

The next and final berg though was the one which posed the greatest problem. It only became visible a couple of miles ahead as dusk was approaching – I had no option other than to go below it, past its **leeward** face, which is the dangerous side. **Growlers** are guaranteed on the downwind side of these bergs, and though I had seen a few scattered around, they had been car-sized and visible. But ahead of me I could see more growlers, and though I sailed as low as I could to miss the berg, and was over a mile from its position, there seemed no avoiding what was ahead of us. The dark sea was strewn with ice, almost like ice-cubes floating in a glass.

Ellen MacArthur, *Taking on the World*

Expand your vocabulary

15 knots – approximately 17 mph
crevasse – deep crack in an iceberg
leeward – side towards which the wind is blowing
growler – relatively small iceberg

Know how to write texts that describe

I am learning to describe a **place** in a lively and interesting way so that I can:

→ choose details that represent the overall impression that I want to give

→ give a sense of mood and atmosphere through my word choices

→ choose words for interest and effect

→ use imagery in an appropriate way.

Your writing task

Describe a journey through familiar places. Start by exploring writing techniques used to describe a writer's real-life experience of a place. Then try out some of the techniques in your own writing. Add annotations and commentary to show off the techniques you are using:

● What I'm trying to do as a writer now …

● Here is an example of …

● I chose these words / phrases because …

● This creates an impression / sense of mood by …

Activity 1 | Select details and choose words and phrases

1 Read the passage opposite, about a sea crossing in the Arctic.

a) What details about the weather does the author choose to describe?

b) What birds and animals does she describe and what are they doing?

c) Find the image the author uses to describe the sea (saying what it is 'like'). How does this make the sea seem? For example, does it sound fierce, dangerous, beautiful, cold?

Activity 2 | Choose descriptive phrases to convey mood or atmosphere

The author makes the experience sound positive and enjoyable. For example, she uses positive phrases for feelings, like 'surge of happiness' and 'glowing with excitement'.

1 Find three other descriptive phrases that the author has chosen to give the impression that the experience was enjoyable and exciting for her and her friends.

2 Write a sentence of your own about an enjoyable experience using a descriptive phrase to express how enjoyable it was.

Activity 3 | Create details, impression and sense of mood in your own writing

1 Describe a journey of your own that is familiar to you. For example, it could be the one to school, or into town.

● Start by planning. First list three details that you could include.

● Then think of phrases that you could use to describe them. Show the reader how you feel about these details in your phrases. They could reflect your mood on the journey.

● Next think of a further detail and think of an image for it that shows what it is like, **and** that fits the mood of your description. For example:

> The huge crane on the building site stood like a gloomy giant, staring down at the children on the swings below.

● Now put your phrases and image together and add to them, to draft some paragraphs describing the journey.

● Remember to edit, redraft and proofread your final draft.

A boat journey

The boat was already desperately low in the water and we packed it carefully, stacking the heavier provisions, fuel and heaters all in the bow to try and push the weight forward. The sun glittered off the water and I felt a surge of happiness to be on the move and to be getting out of the oppressive feel of Qaanaaq.

Visual details suggests mood

Appeal to senses

The journey was long with a biting wind that had us huddling together for warmth, although the boys had to practically hang off the front of the boat to keep the **bow** down to make any progress at all. Baali and Kristian were glowing with excitement, cracking jokes and trying to make the straight-faced boys laugh by pulling silly faces. The water was like a **bolt** of rippling blue-silver silk that had been thrown to the foot of the dark grey mountains, which had been recently dusted lightly with fresh snow. **Guillemots** dived and skimmed the water and tiny black-backed, white-breasted **auklets** bobbed daintily on the small waves. A small pod of seal broke the surface of the water in front of us, somehow aware that we were too overloaded to be interested in them. The sun glinted off their sleek backs as they tumbled playfully in the waters – I felt my spirits soar higher and higher. A single seagull flew directly overhead, all of us watching its low **languid** path, and the quiver of its tail feathers …

Playful behaviour described in light-hearted way

Detailed visual description

Kari Herbert, *The Explorer's Daughter*

Expand your vocabulary

bow – front of boat (rhymes with **cow**)
bolt – a big roll (of material)
guillemots, auklets – seabirds
languid – relaxed, lazy

Your writing task

Write a description that appeals to the reader's senses and brings the experience alive as if it is happening now. First work through the activities to learn how a writer creates the effect of an event happening in 'real time'. Then try out some of the techniques in your own writing.

Add annotations and commentary to show off the techniques you are using:

- What I'm trying to do as a writer now …
- Here is an example of appealing to the readers' senses …
- I chose these words / phrases to convey feelings to …
- I chose these sentence types because …
- I used this tense so that …

I am learning to describe a **personal experience** in a lively and interesting way so that I can:

→ choose words to appeal to the reader's senses

→ structure sentences and use tenses to bring the experience alive, as if it was happening now.

Activity 1   How to appeal to the readers' senses

1 Read the description opposite. It is by a man who paddled a dugout canoe single-handed down a big tidal river in the South American jungle. He is camping for the night and has not been able to get far above river level. How would you sum up how he seems to feel about this camping experience?

2 Which of your five senses does this author appeal to? Start with the example in the opening sentence. Write down at least one phrase from the passage that appeals to each of the senses you have listed.

3 The author chooses his words carefully. Look at these verbs that he uses in the second paragraph, and the less effective words he could have used. Explain how each of the words he has actually used is more effective.

Used	Less effective
rising, inching … lapping	getting
charge	run
chomp	bite
crush	squash
grinding	chewing
dragging	talking

4 The author uses the following adjective in this paragraph: '**jagged** teeth'. He could have used another word, such as 'big' or 'pointy'.
   a) How does his word choice add to the description of what he is afraid will happen to him?
   b) Think of one more adjective that could be added somewhere in this paragraph for the same sort of effect.

Activity 2   How to convey feelings

1 The author uses some short sentences for dramatic effect.
   a) Find three in the first paragraph that do not even have verbs.
   b) How do they help to reveal what the experience was like for him?
2 What questions does the author use, and how do these suggest his mood?
3 The author shows us his feelings by what he does.
   a) List at least three things that he does in the final three paragraphs that reveal his feelings.
   b) Explain how this series of actions shows his feelings.

Camping on a mud flat at night

By midnight I'm sweating and soaked through in my nylon tent. The air is thick and wet and black so that I can hardly breathe. I can't see anything. I wish that a breeze would rustle the trees and drown out these unknowable water noises. These clicks and pops. Branches snapping. The sound of voices. Whose voices? I'm far from any village or any pathway, so why do I hear **machetes** and rifles scraping over a **mangrove** root?

I'm on the highest patch of the mud flat, but the water is still rising, inching higher and higher, until it's lapping at the doorway of the tent. This is just how an alligator or a crocodile wants his supper. He'll charge out with his jaws open, chomp down on the tent with his jagged teeth and crush my body, grinding back and forth while dragging me into the water.

This isn't like **swamping** a dugout canoe in a racing flood current at night. I don't have anything to confront. No wild animal, no thieves in the night, or a Colombian **guerrilla**. There's only my fear, and my unbridled imagination.

Now I hear boots trampling the ground outside. I can't get this madness under control. I fall apart in the tent, trembling and weeping. I can't find my glasses or even my shirt. I pull on my pants. I've

lost the flashlight, but I grab my machete. I tear open the tent zipper and burst through the doorway into the mud and shallow water. Mosquitoes cover my body and face. I raise my machete overhead to attack, to cut someone down, anyone, anything.

I try to roar. I let go with everything I have left, but it gets caught in my throat and warbles. I try a second time to roar like a beast. Still nothing. And nothing answers. Only the mosquitoes in my ears. My heart pounding in my head. Mangroves clicking, more water noises. Everything the same as before.

I fall to my knees in the mud. My tent is full of insects.

Martin Douglas Mitchinson, *A Dugout Canoe in the Darien Gap*

Activity 3	Bring experiences alive as if they are happening now in your own writing

Imagine you are in a difficult situation, perhaps trapped somewhere, or camping somewhere dangerous and unpleasant. List three details you could include in a description, and how you could make your description of them appeal to the senses.

1 Write a paragraph of description using your details.
   - Start by planning.
   - Use a mixture of short and long sentences for dramatic effect.
   - Write in the present tense, like the author above to make the description more immediate.
   - Remember to edit, redraft and proofread your final draft.

Expand your vocabulary

machete – big knife for hacking down jungle, or for use as a weapon
mangrove – tree with spreading roots; grows in swamps
swamping – overturning (a canoe)
guerrilla – armed rebel soldier

I am learning to describe a **person** in a lively and interesting way so that I can:

➡ use adjectives, verbs and adverbs effectively to describe someone's physical appearance

➡ choose details of what someone does to reveal their character

➡ use imagery to show what someone is like.

Your writing task

Write a short descriptive piece in which you introduce and describe a real or imagined person. Start by exploring the techniques that Gerald Durrell uses in the description of Spiro. Then try out some of the techniques in your own writing.

Add annotations and commentary to show off the techniques you are using:

● What I'm trying to do as a writer now …

● Here is an example of revealing character by …

● I chose these words / phrases to …

● I chose this image to show …

● I used this comparison so that …

Activity 1   Reveal character by describing a person's voice

Read Gerald Durrell's description opposite of how his family first met the Greek taxi driver, Spiro, when they went to live on the island of Corfu.

1 Durrell introduces Spiro in the first paragraph with just one detail: his voice. Find the following techniques used to reveal what his voice is like:

a) two verbs

b) three adjectives in a row

c) a comparison (with something else that might have a similar voice).

2 Explain what these three techniques reveal about Spiro's voice.

3 Write an opening paragraph in which you introduce a real or imagined person by describing their voice. Use the same techniques as Durrell.

Activity 2   Reveal character by describing a person's appearance

1 Find and list at least four words or phrases in the second paragraph which reveal:

a) what Spiro looks like

b) how he moves and behaves.

Explain the effect of each word or phrase. For example:

Words or phrases that reveal what Spiro looks like/how he moves and behaves	What the words and phrases suggest about Spiro
surged	This suggests that Spiro is a powerful, energetic force.

2 Add to the description you began in Activity 1 by writing a second paragraph. Use the same techniques as Durrell to reveal character by describing:

a) what this person looks like

b) how they move and behave.

Activity 3   Reveal character by describing what someone does

1 List the things Spiro does for the family.

2 Write a sentence summing up what this shows about Spiro's character.

3 In imaginative writing, how someone sounds and looks can be a clue to their character. What does the phrase 'bull-voiced and scowling' suggest about Spiro's character?

4 Durrell uses two similes in the last paragraph. What two things do these suggest about Spiro's character?

a) '... he stuck to us like a burr.'

b) 'Like a great, brown, ugly angel ...'

5 In the second paragraph, Durrell uses the adverb 'ferociously' to describe how fiercely Spiro scowls. What adverb does Durrell use in the final paragraph to create a very different effect?

Spiro

At that moment everyone was startled into silence by a voice that rumbled out above the uproar, a deep, rich, vibrant voice, the sort of voice you would expect a volcano to have. 'Hoy!' roared the voice, 'whys donts yous have someones who can talks your own language?'

Turning, we saw an ancient **Dodge** parked by the kerb, and behind the wheel sat a short, barrel-bodied individual, with ham-like hands and a great, leathery, scowling face surmounted by a jauntily-tilted peaked cap. He opened the door of the car, surged out onto the pavement, and waddled across to us. Then he stopped, scowling even more ferociously, and surveyed the group of silent cab-drivers.

'Thems been worrying yous?' he asked Mother. ...

Once Spiro had taken charge he stuck to us like a **burr**. Within a few hours he had changed from a taxi-driver to our champion, and within a week he was our guide, philosopher, and friend. He became so much a member of the family that very soon there was scarcely a thing we did, or planned to do, in which he was not involved in some way. He was always there, bull-voiced and scowling, arranging things we wanted done, telling us how much to pay for things, keeping a watchful eye on us all, and reporting to Mother anything he thought she should know. Like a great, brown, ugly angel he watched over us as tenderly as though we were slightly weak-minded children. Mother he **frankly** adored, and he would sing her praises in a loud voice wherever we happened to be, to her **acute** embarrassment.

Gerald Durrell, *My Family and Other Animals*

Activity 4	Describe voice, appearance and action to create character in your own writing

Expand your vocabulary

Dodge – old American-style car
burr – a burr, on a plant, has tiny hooks that cling to clothing
frankly – openly, clearly
acute – high, or extreme

1 Complete your description of a person. Write a final paragraph to show what the person is like, using Durrell's techniques:

- Describe what they do.
- Suggest their character by how they sound and look.
- Use a simile (using 'like' or 'as').
- Add an adverb to a verb to describe **how** they do something, e.g. tenderly.
- Remember to edit, redraft and proofread your final draft.

Know how to write narratives

I am learning how to:

→ create interesting and engaging story openings
→ create strong characters
→ set up dilemmas
→ plan a resolution.

Your writing task

Plan the key elements of a short story. Your plan should include:

- writing an interesting opening
- describing two characters
- planning a dilemma that the characters face
- planning a resolution at the end.

Activity 1 — Consider different kinds of openings

The start of a story needs to interest the reader, so that they are 'hooked in' and want to carry on reading. Here are four effective ways of starting a story.

1 One way of opening is to plunge straight into the action. Read this opening from a short story 'Excuses, Excuses' by Andrew Matthews.

> Not long after the roof blew off Wyvern Copse School, Two Red noticed that there was a battle going on. The battle was between Gerry Atkins and Mr Haggerty, Two Red's French teacher, and it was about homework: or rather the lack of it.

The roof blowing off intrigues the reader

The plot of the story, the battle between the teacher and student, is introduced at the start

2 You could also start in the middle of a conversation. Read this opening from another short story, 'She' by Rosa Guy.

The battle between the daughter and stepmother begins right from the start

> 'Just where do you think you're going?' she said.
>
> 'To the bathroom,' I said.
>
> 'No, you're not,' she said. 'Not before you wash up these dishes.'

The setting in the kitchen is clear

3 You can use description to lead the reader into the heart of the story. Read this extract from 'The Ghost Train' by Sydney J Boulds.

The description of the boy running builds excitement

> Billy Trent ran down the lane towards the common, sandy hair poking like straws from under his cap, his eyes gleaming with excitement. The common blazed with coloured lights, post-box red and dandelion yellow and neon blue. The evening air throbbed with the sound of fairground music and his pulse beat in rhythm.
>
> He reached the entrance and passed beneath the banner that read: BIGGEST TRAVELLING FAIR IN BRITAIN!

The lights and the music show the fairground getting closer as the boy runs

The capital letters add to the sense of anticipation

Each of these very different openings takes the reader into the story quickly and makes them want to read on find out more.

4 Choose one of these ways of beginning a story and write a similar opening for a short story of your own.

Activity 2 | Create interesting characters

Characters can be developed through description and the way they speak.

1 Read this description of Gerry and his teacher from 'Excuses, Excuses'.

> Gerry was a pear-shaped boy with brown hair and freckles whose only outstanding quality was his unremarkability; Mr Haggerty was a large man with a mane of white hair, bristling eyebrows and a reputation for prickliness. He was particularly prickly when it came to homework and was Master of the Awkward Question.
>
> 'I couldn't do the exercise you set us last night, I didn't understand it, sir,' would be met with, 'Then where is the work you did instead?'

The description emphasises the difference between the two characters

The way the characters speak provides more detail about their characters

2 Describe two main characters for the opening of your story. Include some dialogue to show their character or personality by the way they speak.

Activity 3 | Create a dilemma

A dilemma – a problem for the characters – is usually at the heart of a narrative. For example, Billy's dilemma in 'The Ghost Train' begins when two older boys bully him to pay for their rides.

> Ed's big hand tightened on his arm till it throbbed with pain. 'Now come on, share the loot – reckon we'll all go on the dodgems first, okay?'
>
> Billy gasped desperately. 'You're hurting me. All right, I'll pay for you to have one ride, if you promise to leave me alone after that.'

The other example stories in Activity 1 each have different dilemmas.

1 Decide on the dilemma for your story. What problem might your characters have to face?

2 Write the next paragraph of your story, in which the dilemma is introduced.

Activity 4 | Look forward to the ending – the 'resolution'

A 'resolution' of the dilemma creates the ending of many stories.

- In 'Excuses, Excuses', Gerry manages to get his French teacher to agree that he doesn't have to do the extra homework.
- In 'The Ghost Train', Billy Trent manages to get his own back on the two bullies.
- In 'She', the stepmother finally tricks the girl into doing the washing up.

1 Plan the resolution for your own story – where the dilemma or problem for your characters is worked out. Make some notes where you show how you plan the story to end. However, remember that when you actually write it, you may decide to alter how it ends.

13 Know how to write a script for a talk or presentation

I am learning how to write a formal speech by:
→ creating a strong opening
→ using rhetorical devices
→ using a powerful ending.

Your writing task

Write an effective script for a formal speech, basing your approach on what you can learn from an example of a great speech.

Activity 1 Decide on a topic for your own speech

As you work through this section, you will be guided towards writing your own powerful short speech. It needs to be based on a topic or issue that you feel strongly about.

1 Choose your topic and make some brief notes of the key points you want to make.

Activity 2 Write a strong opening

A great speech grabs the attention of an audience with a strong opening.

1 Read this opening from a speech by President Obama on 25 June 2013 on the dangers of climate change.

> The audience will be surprised by the anecdote about space when they know the speech will be about climate change

On Christmas Eve, 1968, the astronauts of *Apollo 8* did a live broadcast from lunar orbit. So Frank Borman, Jim Lovell, William Anders – the first humans to orbit the Moon – described what they saw, and they read Scripture from the Book of Genesis to the rest of us back here. And later that night, they took a photo that would change the way we see and think about our world.

> The links between the anecdote and climate change begin

> Powerful description creates an image for the listeners

It was an image of Earth – beautiful; breathtaking; a glowing marble of blue oceans, and green forests, and brown mountains brushed with white clouds, rising over the surface of the Moon.

And while the sight of our planet from space might seem routine today, imagine what it looked like to those of us seeing our home, our planet, for the first time. Imagine what it looked like to children like me. Even the astronauts were amazed. 'It makes you realise,' Lovell would say, 'just what you have back there on Earth.'

> Emphasises that he saw the photograph as a boy

> The links with the topic of the danger of climate change to the Earth are made clear by the astronaut's final comment

Focus your effort

Remember to include description that creates a powerful image for your audience, and show how your anecdote will link to your topic.

2 Decide on an anecdote to begin your speech. Choose one that links with the topic you chose for your speech.
3 Write the opening paragraph of your speech.

Activity 3   Use convincing details

Using **facts** and **short sentences** are also powerful ways to convince listeners.

> The 12 warmest years in recorded history have all come in the last 15 years. Last year, temperatures in some areas of the ocean reached record highs, and ice in the Arctic shrank to its smallest size on record – faster than most models had predicted it would. These are facts.

Using figures gives the speech authority

'Record highs' and 'smallest size' emphasise the serious situation

A short sentence is used to summarise the point

1 Go back to the opening of your speech. Add some facts and an effective short sentence.

Activity 4   Use rhetorical devices

Rhetorical questions make the listeners think the speaker must be right. **Repetition** reinforces points and **actual examples** help listeners' understanding.

The **rule of three**, where three examples are provided, is a very popular rhetorical device. This is because it sounds really powerful when said out loud.

An actual example is used to illustrate the ideas in the speech

> Walmart is working to cut its carbon pollution by 20 per cent and transition completely to renewable energy. Walmart deserves a cheer for that. But think about it. Would the biggest company, the biggest retailer in America – would they really do that if it weren't good for business, if it weren't good for their shareholders?
>
> A low-carbon, clean energy economy can be an engine of growth for decades to come. And I want America to build that engine. I want America to build that future.
>
> And someday, our children, and our children's children, will look at us in the eye and they'll ask us, did we do all that we could when we had the chance to deal with this problem and leave them a cleaner, safer, more stable world? And I want to be able to say, yes, we did. Don't you want that?

The rhetorical question makes listeners think that Walmart must be right

Repetition reinforces what the President wants to happen

Three examples are used powerfully

A rhetorical question is also used

1 Now add rhetorical questions, repetition, an example and a rule of three to the draft of your speech.

Activity 5   Create a strong ending

Linking back to the **start** of your speech and making a final **summary statement** is a strong way to end a speech. This is how President Obama's ends:

> 'It makes you realise,' that astronaut said all those years ago, 'just what you have back there on Earth.' And that image in the photograph, that bright blue ball rising over the Moon's surface, containing everything we hold dear – the laughter of children, a quiet sunset, all the hopes and dreams of posterity – that's what's at stake. That's what we're fighting for. And if we remember that, I'm absolutely sure we'll succeed.

The link back to the anecdote about the astronauts is a good way to end

The President summarises the importance of the fight

1 Now add a strong ending to your speech, linking back to the start.

Know how to use the conventions of a play script

I am learning how to write effective play scripts by:

→ setting out my play script in the correct format

→ using stage directions to describe setting, mood and character

→ indicating events and how characters should move and speak.

Activity 1 | Set out a play script

Play scripts conform to a particular set format, usually with the speaker's name on the left in capital letters or bold, and what they say on the right. Look at how William Shakespeare does this in *Macbeth*.

> **Act 1 Scene 1 An open place**
>
> *Thunder and lightning. Enter three witches.*
>
> **First Witch:**   When shall we three meet again?
>
>   In thunder, lightning or in rain?
>
> **Second Witch:** When the hurlyburly's done,
>
>   When the battle's lost and won.
>
> **Third Witch:**   That will be ere the set of sun.

1 Here is the next part of the scene from *Macbeth*. This time, it is not set out in the proper format. Rewrite the extract into the correct play-script format.

> 'Where the place?' said the First Witch. 'Upon the heath', replied the Second Witch. 'There to meet with Macbeth' volunteered the Third Witch. 'I come, Graymalkin!' cried the First Witch.

Activity 2 | Include stage directions

Stage directions are an important part of a play script. They are usually indicated in italic text. Look again at the start of *Macbeth*. The stage directions *'An open place'* and *'Thunder and lightning. Enter three witches'* indicate the setting and mood, and that the scene is set in an open place in a storm.

Stage directions are also used to describe the appearance of characters and how they should speak.

1 Read the opening on the opposite page from *The Play of Kes* by Barry Hines and Allan Stronach. The script is based on the novel *A Kestrel for a Knave*. In the novel, the writer can describe what happens. In the play script, stage directions are used to indicate events and characters' actions.

Billy Casper shares a bedroom with his older brother Jud. Billy is in his last year at school, while Jud works as a miner in the local coal pit. This scene is from the beginning of the script. It is early morning, and Billy and Jud are both asleep.

> The stage directions explain the opening scene

(Billy and Jud's bedroom and kitchen. Billy and Jud are asleep. Quiet. The alarm clock rings. Billy fumbles for it, eventually finds it and switches it off.)

> The alarm clock going off on the silent stage surprises the audience and Billy

Billy: Bloody thing. *(Pause)* Jud! *(Pause)*

Jud: What?

Billy: You'd better get up. *(Pause)* Alarm's gone off you know.

> Billy's attempts to wake Jud are indicated by the pauses

Jud: Think I don't know? *(Pause)*

Billy: Jud.

Jud: What?

Billy: You'll be late.

Jud: Oh, shut it.

> Billy's style of speaking is made clear by the way the speech is written

Billy: Clock's gone off you know.

Jud: I said 'shut it!' *(He thumps Billy)*

Billy: Gi'oer, that hurts.

Jud: Well, shut it then.

Billy: I'll tell mi' mam about you.

(Jud slowly gets out of bed. He finally finds his trousers and puts them on.)

Activity 3 Write the next section of the scene from *The Play of Kes*

This is how the novel tells what happens next:

Billy snuggled down in Jud's place, making the springs creak. Jud looked at the humped blankets, then walked across and pulled then back, stripping the bed completely … For an instant Billy lay curled up, his hands wafered between his thighs. Then he sat up and crawled to the bottom of the bed to retrieve the blankets.

'You rotten sod, just because tha's to get up.'

'Another few weeks, lad, an' tha'll be getting up wi' me. '

He walked to the end of the landing. Billy propped himself up on one elbow.

'Switch t'light out, then!'

1 Rewrite this as the next section of the play script.

Focus your effort

Set out the script like the examples above. Add stage directions to show how the characters speak and move and to describe events. Use the actual words that the characters speak.

You can't include all of the description in the novel. Decide what to include as stage directions, and what to leave out. Use the present tense for directions.

Know how to write recounts

I am learning how to write effective recounts that:

➜ give readers all the necessary information

➜ use the first person and the past tense.

Your writing task

Write a recount of an event in your life. Your recount should:

● include precise details as well as your thoughts and feelings

● be written in the past tense and use the first person.

A **recount** is a non-fiction text that tells the facts or the true story of something. It is usually told using the past tense, and in chronological (time) sequence. Recounts include newspaper articles, accounts of events by scientists, inventors, explorers and travellers, and personal recounts in diaries and autobiographies.

Activity 1 | Write a short news recount

News articles in newspapers or online are often recounts. They tell the reader:

● what happened

● where the event took place

● when the event happened

● who was involved.

1 Read the newspaper article opposite. Look at the features which make it an effectively written recount.

2 Here are some facts about the recent sale of a book for charity. Use these facts to write a short recount paragraph in continuous prose, using the correct tense, pronouns and connectives.

● A copy of the book *Harry Potter and the Philosopher's Stone* was sold for £150 000.

● It was sold in London on Tuesday, 21 May.

● The sale was for charity.

● It was sold at Sotheby's.

● J. K. Rowling had written notes in the copy about how she wrote it.

● People were surprised it fetched so much money.

● There are 22 drawings by J. K. Rowling in the book.

● The sale was for the charity PEN, which helps writers.

Rescuers pull 58 charity swimmers from the sea

What happened is explained.

When the event took place is included.

Who was involved is explained.

The places where the event happened are mentioned.

More details of what happened are given later in the article.

Rescue teams pulled dozens of swimmers from choppy seas yesterday as a charity race descended into chaos. Up to 90 of the 130 entrants were unaccounted for at one point as a major air and sea operation was launched to rescue those in difficulty off the coast of Suffolk.

Deteriorating conditions and rough waters left many competitors in the 1.2 km Southwold pier to pub swim, some of them novices, unable to cope. After an hour, emergency services were called in. Five lifeboats and an RAF helicopter were scrambled at 4pm. Three people were taken to Paget university hospital in Great Yarmouth with suspected hypothermia, the coastguard said.

A lifeboat hut near the pier served as a makeshift emergency centre as bedraggled swimmers were dried off and treated. A coastguard spokeswoman said rescue boats pulled 58 people out of the water, while some swam to shore.

One entrant, who was rescued by a boat crew, said it was 'like swimming on a treadmill' and after an hour's effort she had ended up north of where she began, having intended to swim south.

An interview with one of the people rescued is included.

Everyone pulled from the water was conscious and there were no reported fatalities, the spokeswoman said.

By Mark Taylor

Activity 2 | Write a recount of an event

When you write about something you have experienced or done this is a **personal** recount. If it is an important event it is necessary to include precise details to prove it really happened.

1 Read this account of the first powered flight in 1903 by two brothers, Orville and Wilbur Wright:

> During the night of 16th December a strong cold wind blew from the north. When we rose on the morning of the 17th, the puddles of water, which had been standing about camp since the recent rains, were covered with ice. The wind had a velocity of 22 to 27 miles per hour. We thought it would die down before long, but when 10 o'clock arrived, and the wind was as brisk as ever, we decided that we had better get the machine out. Wilbur, having used his turn in the unsuccessful attempt on the 14th, the right to the first trial fell to me. Wilbur ran at the side, holding the wings to balance it on the track. The machine, facing a 27-mile per hour wind, started very slowly. Wilbur was able to stay with it until it lifted ponderously from the track after a forty foot run.
>
> The course of the flight up and down was exceedingly erratic. The control of the front rudder was difficult. As a result, the machine would rise suddenly to about ten feet and then as suddenly dart for the ground. A sudden dart when a little over 120 feet from the point at which it rose in the air, ended the flight.
>
> This flight lasted only twelve seconds, but it was nevertheless the first in the history of the world …

Dates and time are included to prove it happened

The recount describes exactly what happened.

Because this is a recount of a scientific event, precise details are recorded

Formal recounts also need precise information. They are written **objectively** – in other words they cut out any personal thoughts and feelings and aim to present the facts as they happened. For example, a witness statement about a crime is a formal recount.

2 The following recount by a witness to a crime is not precise enough. Use the facts listed below to rewrite it to include precise details of the time, the place and exactly what happened. Make the account **objective**.

Witness statement

I went to my bank in the town the other day during the morning. As I went through the front door I heard a shout and someone rushed past. The person was medium height. The person ran off towards the station. I could see that the people in the bank were upset. I tried to see where the person had gone but I couldn't see after he had gone round the corner. I called the police.

Facts

- Date: Wednesday, 30 January
- Time: 10:23 a.m.
- Place: Co-op bank in Hale Road, Hythe
- The criminal: the man was around 40 years old
- Height: 5 ft 7 inches tall
- Clothing: black shirt, dark trousers and carrying a red bag
- The criminal ran towards: Hythe Station
- People in the bank: customers were in shock
- The bank staff: employees were trying to help them
- The criminal ran to: corner of the High Street
- Witness's action: I rang the police on my mobile.

> **Focus your effort**
>
> - Think about what details to include and what to leave out.
> - Write in the third person.
> - Write a first draft then review it so you can improve.

Activity 3   Personal recount

1 Read this recount of a ballooning disaster by Sir Richard Branson, the famous entrepreneur.

After crossing the Atlantic Ocean in a balloon, ropes have become tangled and the balloon is falling toward the sea. Sir Richard's pilot, Per Lindstrom, has already jumped into the sea. Now, Sir Richard has to decide when to jump.

I was fifty feet away, the height of a house, and the sea was rushing up to hit me. I checked my life jacket and held on to the railing. Without my weight, I hoped the balloon would rise up again rather than crashing on top of me. I waited until I was just above the sea before pulling my life-jacket ripcord and hurling myself away from the capsule.

The sea was icy. I spun deep into it and felt my scalp freeze with the water. Then the life jacket bobbed me straight back up to the surface. It was heaven: I was alive. I turned and watched the balloon. Without my weight, it quietly soared back up through the cloud like a magnificent alien spaceship, vanishing from sight.

The helicopter flew over me and lowered a sling. I sat inside it like a swing, but each time it tried to lift me it dunked me back in the water. I couldn't understand what was wrong, and I was too weak to hold on much longer. Eventually it winched me up and someone reached out and pulled me inside.

'You should have put the sling under your arms,' said a Scottish voice.

2 This is a well-written personal account of the rescue. Rewrite it as one of the following:

- A newspaper report. You may wish to add details, for example, an interview with one or more of the participants. Use 180–200 words.
- A witness statement, for example, from the helicopter pilot or winchman. Use 100–150 words.

Assess your progress – writing to inform or explain

Your writing task

Think of a subject that you know more about than some people do, such as a band, a sport, a TV series or your school.

1 Write an informative article on the subject for someone who does not know much about it (for example, a new pupil at your school).

2 Present the information in an interesting and helpful way.

Word count: around 200–250 words   **Number of paragraphs:** around 1–3

Add annotations and commentary to point out the techniques you are using.

For example:

- Here I'm trying to …
- Here is an example of …
- I chose these words because …
- I chose these sentence types because …

Remind yourself of some techniques that writers use to inform or explain. Read the article opposite, about exercising to music. Then read the annotations to explore what techniques it uses.

Plan, draft, edit and proofread

- Plan your writing. Use a method that works for you, for example, a mind map, spidergram or bullet points.
- Think about the key information you need to give, and anything you need to explain.
- Think about a heading, how to introduce the subject, how to order the information, and how to end. Will you need subheadings?
- Write an opening sentence summing up what readers will learn.
- Use your plan to draft the rest of the article. You could use some of the techniques used opposite.
- Read through and edit your draft to make improvements. What words or phrases could you improve? How could you improve your language so it is original and interesting as well as grammatically correct?
- Make sure you have stuck to the present tense, unless you are explaining background, as in 'In the old days, players used to …'
- Proofread your draft for accurate spelling and punctuation. Make sure you have started new sentences and paragraphs where necessary.

 Now turn to pages 160–161 to track your progress in writing.

Running to music

Previews what the feature is about

Named expert – gives us faith in the information

Q&A – helpful technique

Clear, straightforward language

Backs up information with statistic

Explains using dash

Music can help you run more efficiently and for longer, according to research. Sport and exercise expert Professor Andrew Lane talks about music's performance-enhancing qualities.

What effect does music have on us?

Music can influence our state of mind. Not only can it enhance our mood, it can also change our mood. It can relax and it can energise. Music can act as a companion to whatever activity you're engaging in, from reading to exercising. If you can match the tempo of the music with the activity, it can improve your enjoyment of that activity.

How can music help running?

Music can trick your mind into feeling less tired during a workout, especially repetitive movement exercises such as running. Research suggests that listening to music while exercising can reduce perceptions of effort and fatigue by up to 12 per cent. If you're listening to music while running, it can distract you from the actual effort of running – you are listening to the beat of a song rather than the thump coming from your heartbeat.

Does that mean I'm likely to run for longer?

By reducing your feeling of tiredness, you are more likely to go on for longer. What's more, research suggests that if you keep in step with the music, your stride will be more rhythmical and therefore more efficient. Tests on walkers found that walking in time to a musical beat improved endurance by 15 per cent.

'Signpost' word explains effect

Assess your progress – writing summaries

Your writing task

Read the passage opposite, about Liverpool, and the summary of the second paragraph.

1 Make a bullet point list of the main information in the first paragraph.
2 Turn your list into a continuous summary, using your own words where possible.

Word count: 75–90 words   **Number of paragraphs:** 1–2

Add annotations and commentary to show off the techniques you are using.

For example:

- Here I've …
- Here is an example of …
- I reworded this because …
- I chose this sentence type because …

Remind yourself of some techniques that writers use to summarise. Read the article opposite, about Liverpool. Then read the summary of the second paragraph. Read the annotations on both to explore the summarising techniques.

Plan, draft, edit and proofread

- Plan your writing by listing the main points to include. Use a method that works for you, for example, a mind map, spidergram or bullet points.
- Think about what information you could leave out.
- Think about the best order for your summary.
- Use your plan to draft the rest of the summary. You could use some of the techniques used opposite.
- Read through and edit your draft to make improvements. What words or phrases could you improve? How could you make it flow more smoothly?
- Proofread your final draft for accurate spelling and punctuation. Make sure you have started new sentences and paragraphs where necessary.

Now turn to pages 162–163 to track your progress in writing.

Liverpool

Standing proud in the 1700s as the empire's second city, Liverpool faced a dramatic change in fortune in the twentieth century, suffering a series of harsh economic blows and ongoing urban deprivation. The postwar years were particularly tough, with the battered city becoming a byword for British economic malaise, but the outlook changed again at the turn of the millennium, as economic and social regeneration brightened the centre and old docks, and the city's stint as European Capital of Culture in 2008 transformed the view from outside. Today Liverpool is a dynamic, exciting place: it's a vibrant city with a Tate Gallery of its own, a series of innovative museums and a fascinating social history. And of course it also makes great play of its musical heritage – as well it should, considering that this is the place that gave the world The Beatles.

The main sights are scattered throughout the centre of town, but you can easily walk between most of them. The River Mersey provides one focus, whether crossing on the famous ferry to the Wirral peninsula or taking a tour of the Albert Dock. Beatles sights could easily occupy another day. If you want a cathedral, they've 'got one to spare' as the song goes; plus there's a fine showing of British art in the celebrated Walker Art Gallery and Tate Liverpool, a multitude of exhibits in the terrific World Museum Liverpool, and a revitalized arts and nightlife urban quarter centred on FACT, Liverpool's showcase for film and the media arts.

Unnecessary detail

Fun, but long-winded

We can take this for granted

Part of media

Expand your vocabulary

malaise – sickness

Summary of second paragraph

Liverpool's main sights are all within walking distance of the centre. You can cross the Mersey on the ferry or take a tour of the Albert Dock. There are also the Beatles sites and two cathedrals to see, as well as art galleries, the World Museum Liverpool, and an arts and nightlife area around the FACT media centre.

Reworded concisely

Just main points

Interpreted in fewer words

Names replaced with plural phrase

Concisely reworded

Assess your progress – writing instruction texts

1 Write step-by-step instructions on how to do **one** of the following:
- Tie and untie a tie or a shoe lace
- Make a cup of tea, or a simple meal of your choice
- Log in to your school computer network
- Use your school lunch system

2 Present the information in a concise and helpful way.

3 Use a small number of diagrams or illustrations if necessary.

Word count: around 100–150 words

Number of paragraphs: around 4–9, depending on number of steps needed

Add annotations and commentary to show off the techniques you are using.

For example:
- Here I'm trying to …
- Here is an example of …
- I chose these words because …
- I chose this sentence type because …

Remind yourself of some techniques that writers use in instructions. Read the page opposite, from the HTC Wildfire phone instructions. Then read the annotations to explore what techniques it uses.

Plan, draft, edit and proofread

- Plan your writing. Use a method that works for you, for example, a flow chart, spidergram or bullet points.
- Think about the key information you need to give, and anything you need to explain.
- Think about how to order the information, and how you will deal with options or different preferences. Will you need headings?
- Write an opening sentence summing up what users can do.
- Use your plan to draft the rest of the instructions. You could use some of the techniques used opposite.
- Read through and edit your draft. What words or phrases could you improve? How could you improve your language so it is clear as well as grammatically correct?
- Proofread your draft for accurate spelling and punctuation. Make sure you have started new sentences and paragraphs where necessary, and ordered the steps correctly.

Now turn to pages 164–165 to track your progress in writing.

Rearranging or hiding application tabs

You can rearrange the tabs at the bottom of some apps to prioritize the types of information you frequently use or remove the tabs you don't really need.

1. Open an app that has the usual tabs at the bottom of its screen (for example, the library screen in Music).

2. Press and hold a tab. When the screen changes and shows you an empty area, lift your finger.

3. Do any of the following:

Move a tab	Press and hold the tab you want to move, and then drag it to its new position.
Remove a tab	Press and hold a tab you want to hide, then drag it up. When you see a colored box, lift your finger.

4. When you're done, press ←.

Adding a tab back

1. Open the app from which you previously removed some tabs.

2. Press and hold a tab. When the screen changes and shows you some of your hidden tabs, lift your finger.

3. Press and hold the tab you want to show, then drag it down to where you want to position it again.

    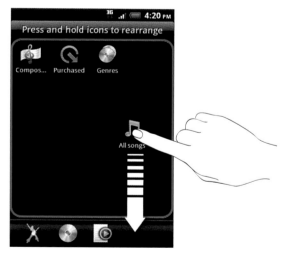

4. When you're done, press ←.

Assess your progress – writing to persuade

Your writing task

Think of something you feel strongly about and want to have changed or stopped.

1 Write an appeal persuading people to sign a petition or donate money to a cause you feel strongly about – such as saving tigers.

2 Use a range of persuasive techniques to ensure that your view on the subject you have selected is conveyed powerfully, and that the reader is likely to be persuaded to act in some way.

Word count: around 180–240 words   **Number of paragraphs:** around 2–4

Add annotations and commentary to show off the techniques you are using.
For example:

- Here I'm trying to …
- Here is an example of …
- I chose these words because …
- I chose these sentence types because …

Remind yourself of some persuasive writing techniques. Read the email appeal opposite. Then read the annotations to explore what techniques it uses.

Plan, draft, edit and proofread

- Plan your writing. Use a method that works for you, for example, a mind map, spidergram or bullet points.
- Think about the main information you want to provide, and anything you need to explain.
- Think about how to introduce the subject, how to order your points, and how to end. Will you need headings?
- Write an opening sentence that grabs the readers' attention.
- Use your plan to draft the rest of the appeal. You could use some of the techniques used opposite, and some similarly emotive language.
- Read through and edit your draft to make improvements. What words or phrases could you improve? How could you improve your language so it is powerfully persuasive as well as grammatically correct?
- Make sure you have really appealed to the reader, using the pronouns 'you' and 'we' effectively.
- Proofread your draft for accurate spelling and punctuation. Make sure you have started new sentences and paragraphs where necessary.

Now turn to pages 166–167 to track your progress in writing.

One tycoon, a whale massacre and dog food

Avaaz.org petition appeal

Announces subject in an exciting, positive way

Another reason to save them

Suggests rich man and irresponsible friends having 'fun'

Strongly critical adjective

Explanatory 'topic sentence'

Strong verb

Strong, emotive noun

'Call to action' using 'we' to include reader

Reminds us why they are worth saving

Contrasts positive appeal with negative

Fin whales are magical giants of the sea. But in days, over 180 of this endangered species are set to be slaughtered by one tycoon and his buddies whose summer hobby is to harpoon them, chop them up and ship their meat through the Netherlands to Japan for dog food!

There is one way to stop the hunt before it starts – you can't dock a boat full of illegal whale carcasses just anywhere. German and Finnish authorities have shunned the shameful trade. Now, the Dutch are the linchpin. They care deeply about their reputation as environmental leaders, and are hoping this bloody trade won't get any global attention. But if we expose it now and demand the Dutch authorities refuse the transfer of whale meat in their port, we can stop the whale massacre!

We have to act fast – the whaling ships are due to start the hunt in days. Sign now and tell everyone to join – let's build a one million strong campaign to Prime Minister Mark Rutte now warning him that we will create a media storm with giant whales on his doorstep unless he stops the transfer in Dutch docks.

These majestic creatures are the second largest animal on earth, they can grow to be as long as three buses and move through water like lightning. Their incredible combination of sleek, elegant power and speed earned them the nickname 'greyhound of the sea'.

Tragically, whalers like Kristjan Loftsson have slaughtered hundreds of thousands and over 70% of the global population was wiped out. … We can help them back from the brink if we stop them from being butchered for dog food!

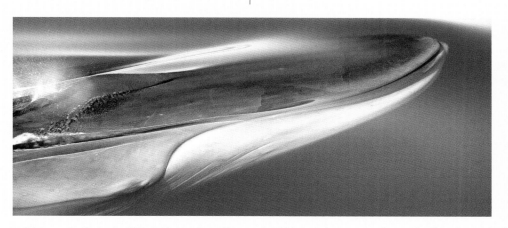

Assess your progress – writing an expository or narrative essay

Describe how you faced a challenge on one day of your life and explain what made it significant.

1 Tell the story of this event in an appealing way.
2 Use language to show your feelings at the time.

Word count: around 200–250 words   **Number of paragraphs:** around 3–4

Add annotations and commentary to show off the techniques you are using.

For example:

- Here I'm trying to …
- Here is an example of …
- I chose these words because …
- I chose these sentence types because …

Remind yourself of some techniques that writers use in this kind of personal writing. Read the true-life account opposite. Then read the annotations to explore what techniques bring it to life for the reader.

Plan, draft, edit and proofread

- Plan your writing. Use a method that works for you, for example, a mind map, spidergram or bullet points.
- Think about the key information you need to give, and how to explain why the event was significant.
- Think about how to tell the story, how to order the information, and how to end.
- Write an opening sentence that sets the scene or somehow catches the reader's attention.
- Use your plan to draft the rest of your account. You could use some of the techniques used opposite, and some words that suggest how you felt at the time.
- Read through and edit your draft to make improvements. What words or phrases could you improve? How could you improve your language so it is original and interesting as well as grammatically correct?
- Make sure you have stuck to the past tense, unless you are explaining, as in 'Generally, I assume …'
- Proofread your draft for accurate spelling and punctuation. Make sure you have started new sentences and paragraphs where necessary.

Now turn to pages 168–169 to track your progress in writing.

Experience: I saved a baby who fell from a window

On a mild October evening, I walked down a busy London street in search of a cashpoint, pausing briefly to look at a menu in a restaurant window.

> Sets scene – everything normal

As I turned from the window, I felt the strangest sensation, like a pigeon flying too close to my head – a rush of air, a sudden movement in my peripheral vision.

> Uses simile and describes actual sensation

Then there was a dull thud on the pavement to my right. I looked down. At first I couldn't comprehend what was there. A pile of rags? No, wait, a doll. To my horror, I realised it was a baby. I looked up, trying to make sense of this awful, totally random event, and saw an open sash window.

> Sense appeal

> Replays his thoughts

My initial reaction was that she must be dead – she was so still and her eyes were closed. I looked around to see if anyone was going to act. No one materialised.

> Dramatic short sentence

Then came the lurching realisation that it was down to me. Generally I assume that there's always someone more skilled, more instinctive than me to take control in a crisis, but we were alone on the street.

> How he felt

In a moment of utter focus, I looked at the tiny child dressed in a pale pink babygrow and everything turned to cinematic slow motion. It felt as if she and I were the only two people in the world. I fumbled for my phone and rang 999 while shouting to the now-gathering crowd to search the many nearby restaurants for a doctor or a nurse. I lay down next to the baby.

> Shares actual experience

> Vivid verb choice

I had done a first-aid course a few months earlier and was grateful for it as I gently checked for a pulse. It was there, and a finger above her mouth confirmed she was breathing.

> Explaining

6 Assess your progress – writing to describe

Your writing task

Describe an outdoor place that you know well for a book in which local people write about where they live. It could be, for example, a garden, a park, a street, a playground or games area, or a riverbank. Make up some of the details if you wish.

1 Make it come alive for readers who do not know it.
2 Give some idea of how you feel about the place by the language you use.

Word count: around 150–200 words   **Number of paragraphs:** around 1–3

Add annotations and commentary to show off the techniques you are using, for example:

- Here I'm trying to …
- Here is an example of …
- I chose these words because …
- I chose these sentence types because …

Remind yourself of some techniques that writers use when creating a description in words. Read the description opposite, of a garden and the creatures living in it. Then read the annotations to explore what makes the place come to life for the reader.

Plan, draft, edit and proofread

- Plan your writing. Use a planning method that works well for you, for example, a mind map, spidergram or bullet points.
- How will you structure your writing? Think about the opening, development and conclusion.
- Write an opening sentence summing up the place in an interesting way.
- Use your plan to draft the rest of the description. You could use some of the techniques used by Durrell, and some words that suggest how you feel about the place.
- Read through and edit your draft to make improvements. What words or phrases could you improve? How could you improve your language so it is original and interesting as well as grammatically correct?
- Make sure you have stuck to either the past tense or the present tense.
- Proofread your draft for accurate spelling and punctuation. Make sure you have started new sentences and paragraphs where necessary.

Now turn to pages 170–171 to track your progress in writing.

What do you know about … the author?

Gerald Durrell was an animal expert who worked with zoos and in conservation. His book *My Family and Other Animals* is based on his time living on the Greek island of Corfu, aged 10–14.

Gives a first impression: garden is small but somehow a whole country

This dolls-house garden was a magic land, a forest of flowers through which roamed creatures I had never seen before. Among the thick, silky petals of each rose-bloom lived tiny, crab-like spiders that scuttled sideways when disturbed. Their small, translucent bodies were coloured to match the flowers they inhabited: pink, ivory, wine-red, or buttery-yellow. On the rose-stems, encrusted with green flies, lady-birds moved like newly painted toys; lady-birds pale red with large black spots; lady-birds apple-red with brown spots; lady-birds orange with grey-and-black freckles. Rotund and amiable, they prowled and fed among the anaemic flocks of greenfly. Carpenter bees, like furry, electric-blue bears, zigzagged among the flowers, growling fatly and busily. Humming-bird hawk-moths, sleek and neat, whipped up and down the paths with a fussy efficiency, pausing occasionally on speed-misty wings to lower a long, slender proboscis into a bloom.

Gerald Durrell, *My Family and Other Animals*

Appeals to sense of touch

Interesting verb choice

Vivid colours

Simile – fun, and goes with 'dolls-house' in the opening sentence

Repetition of 'lady-birds' gives sense of variety

Interesting adjective (pale, bloodless)

Sense appeal: sound effect

Unusual, vivid simile

Unusual adjective ('misty' because moving so fast)

Assess your progress – writing the opening of a story

Now turn to pages 172–173 to track your progress in writing.

Your writing task

Write the opening paragraphs of a story about a challenge between two young people. The challenge can take the form of a race, a trial of strength, playing a game like chess, or you can decide a challenge of your own.

1 Make the opening paragraphs engaging so that the reader wants to carry on reading.

2 Use effective language to create a believable setting for the story.

3 Introduce the main characters and their challenge.

Word count: around 150–200 words   **Number of paragraphs:** 2–3

Add annotations and commentary to demonstrate the techniques you are using, for example:

- Here I'm trying to …
- Here is an example of …
- I chose these words because …
- I chose these sentence types because …

Remind yourself of some techniques that writers use when opening a story. Read the opening paragraphs of two stories on the opposite page which use different ways of interesting the reader. Both stories have a conflict between characters. Then read the annotations to explore what makes them an effective opening for a story.

Plan, draft, edit and proofread

- Plan your writing. Use a planning method that works well for you, such as a mind map, thought diagram or bullet points.
- How will you structure your writing? Think about the opening and how you will develop the challenge.
- Write an opening sentence that will interest your readers.
- Use your plan to draft the rest of the paragraphs. You could use some of the techniques used in the example story.
- Read through and edit your draft to make improvements. What words or phrases could you improve? How could you improve your language so it is original and interesting as well as grammatically correct?
- Make sure you have stuck to either the past tense or the present tense.
- Proofread your draft for accurate spelling and punctuation. Make sure you have started new sentences and paragraphs where necessary.

The opening paragraphs of *Chicken* by Mary Hoffman grabs a reader's interest by introducing several facts about a gang.

The story starts by giving the reader impression that they are in the middle of an intriguing discussion about the gang.

The reference to someone called Mark Mason being 'frozen out' gives an intriguing glimpse of a difficult past for the gang.

It was hard to say when the group became a gang. Perhaps it was when Mark Mason tried to hang around with us and we froze him out. Or perhaps when we started calling ourselves The Inliners. Definitely, we were a gang by the time of the leadership struggle or there wouldn't have been a struggle and we'd never have been so stupid as to do the dares.

The naming of the gang gives the reader another impression of the gang's development.

The words 'leadership struggle' introduce the main theme of the story that there is going to be a struggle between characters.

We had all known each other since Nursery. Alfie and I had hung out together since before we were born actually, because our mums were best friends and they'd gone into hospital to have us on the same day.

The second paragraph fills in the background of the two main characters.

The words 'stupid' and 'the dares' make the readers keen to find out about what happened.

Dylan, Jamal and Leon all live within a couple of streets of Alfie and me. (I'm Rick by the way.) We all learnt to swim together in the local kiddie pool, we all went to birthday parties at each other's houses dressed as Power Rangers or Ninja turtles, all went up to the Juniors at the same time, all played football on the common, all went to Woodcraft and went camping together, all got our first inline skates the same Christmas.

The third paragraph describes all the things they did together when they were younger.

Another story, *Poinsettias* by Beverley Naidoo, uses a different way of interesting the reader, starting with a dramatic moment.

The story begins with a dramatic moment as the glass jar with the snake is pushed towards Marika.

Marika thrust the glass jar up to Veronica's face.

'See this one Nicky!' she declared. 'Caught it last week!' Veronica stared at the coiled brown shape slithering inside the liquid. She felt sick.

The exclamation mark shows Marika is emphasising 'poisonous' to frighten Veronica.

'You should have seen how blinking quick I was man! This sort are poisonous!'

'Slithering' adds to the sense of horror Marika feels as she sees the dead snake.

Marika's eyes pinned her down, watching for a reaction. She didn't know which were worse, Marika's or those of the dead creature in the jar.

'Where did you find it?'

The word 'betray' shows that Veronica didn't want to show Marika that she is frightened.

Her voice did not betray her and Marika began her dramatic tale about tracking the snake in the bougainvillea next to the hen run.

'Pinned down' shows that Marika is trying to frighten Veronica – she is treating her like an insect in an experiment.

The next paragraph explains Marika's interest in collecting and preserving animals.

It was a valuable addition to her collection. Rows of bottles, all with the same green liquid, lined the shelf above her bed. Spiders and insects of various shapes and sizes floated safely, serenely, inside. Marika carefully replaced the snake next to another prize item – a one-legged chameleon its colours dulled and fixed. Veronica remembered it alive. It had been the farm children's pet briefly until they had tired of capturing flies for it.

The comparison between the dead snake's eyes and Marika's eyes shows that Veronica dislikes Marika.

8 Assess your progress – writing a recount

Your writing task

Write a recount of an event in your life. This could be an event at a school, a festival, fair or circus in the area, or a dramatic event like an accident. You can base your account on a true event, or invent one yourself. Decide whether your writing will be for a local newspaper or an online news site. You can invent details such as names of people involved, the names of places and other details like dates and times.

1   Give the readers the important information about: who, where, when, why and how.
2   Remember you are writing for a local audience so include information that is likely to appeal to locals who know the area.

Word count: around 150–200 words   **Number of paragraphs:** around 1–3

Add annotations and commentary to draw attention to the techniques you are using, for example:

- Here I'm trying to …
- Here is an example of …
- I chose these words because …
- I chose these sentence types because …

Remind yourself of some techniques that writers use when writing a recount for a newspaper or online news site. Read the example of a recount on the page opposite. Then read the annotations to find out what makes this a successful example of a newspaper recount.

Plan, draft, edit and proofread

- Plan your writing. Use a planning method that works well for you, for example, a mind map, thought diagram or bullet points.
- How will you structure your writing? Think about the opening where you give the key facts, the development where you provide factual details and a conclusion summing up the event.
- Write an opening paragraph.
- Use your plan to draft the rest of the recount. You could use some of the techniques used in the example recount to make your writing appeal to readers.
- Read through and edit your draft to make improvements. What words or phrases could you improve? How could you improve your language so it interests the readers as well as being grammatically correct?
- Make sure you have stuck to the past tense because a recount tells readers something that has already happened.
- Proofread your final draft for accurate spelling and punctuation. Make sure you have started new sentences and paragraphs where necessary.

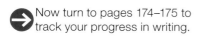
Now turn to pages 174–175 to track your progress in writing.

The words 'hollered' and 'delighted' show the writer's excitement about seeing the killer whales swimming beside their boat.

The description of the fins is detailed with the colour and shiny quality described.

The size of the fins is made clear through the comparison with the height of a man.

The description of the way the killer whales move and the colour of their sides are described very carefully.

The writer remembers the way the next two whales swimming closely together made her think they were mother and young.

Tim was onto the killer whales as soon as I hollered, as soon as I leaned over and thumped him, delighted, yelling about fins. Three fins were clear of the water now, jet-black and sheeny, the male's on the outside so tall, as tall as a man, that the sun dazzled off it. With a slow sea motion they rolled up, fin first, then backs so broad that the sea water spilled off on either side, then we saw their near sides, a medley of white and black. As those three tilted back down in unison, Tim swung to sit beside me, calling, 'Two more, just behind!' And indeed, two more fins, shorter and more hooked than the male's, were appearing up through the water's surface. There was something about that second pair, a collusion or privacy, which made me wonder if they were mother and young. Then they in turn blew, and began to roll under the

surface, and the water closed over them as if they'd never been.

For a few moments there was only sea, and gannets passing below us, with outstretched necks. Then, farther along rightwards, and side by side, the first three fins began to rise again, appearing from underwater into the visible world of light and birds.

Tim said a party of gannets appeared to be following the animals, as gulls follow the plough, and it was so, but the gannets, lately so impressive, suddenly seemed flappy, airy little things, next to the orca's greater presence. And exposed: the killer whales revealed only as much of themselves as necessary; much more of their bodies remained concealed from us under the sea's surface, even when they blew, but the birds were all there, all visible.

'Sightlines' by *Kathleen Jamie*

The next paragraph has precise description of how and where the killer whales reappear.

The writer emphasises the size of the orca (killer whale) by comparing them to the gannets which are large sea birds but now appear small 'airy little things' next to the killer whales.

The fact that most of the killer whales' bodies are hidden from us is emphasised by contrast with the way we can easily see the birds.

Assess your progress – writing to inform or explain

When you have completed **writing to inform or explain** using pages 144–145, use the guide below to track your progress.

> **Assess your description against the examples**
> - Read the descriptions and comments.
> - Is your writing closer to the qualities of Text 1, or Text 2?

Text 1 My village

Could be left out

Good verb choice

The village where I live is not that great but I'm sort of used to it. It is called St Lucy's and it is on a hill overlooking a river. There is not much to do but there is some interesting things, like it has a small castle which was destroyed in the Civil War. It also has a lot of old houses like the village pub. It is meant to be about 400 years old and looks it, with a huge fireplace and heavy dark oak beams.

'Damaged'?

Comma needed

Good description

Should be 'were'

Comma splice

There is a village hall which has events sometimes, like we had a hypnotist once who made people do mad things like thinking they was Elvis Presley. There are also concerts and a youth night with ping pong and other games. There are not many buses – only two a day. So you really need to have a car, the other thing is that the internet is very slow.

Good use of a dash to expand information

One of the most interesting things is St Lucy's Church, which is even older than the pub. It has some dead Vikings buried in the graveyard from a Viking raid, and some unusual carvings of animals on the seats. You can see three counties from the top of the tower.

Good use of subordinated sentence

Overall comment on Text 1

Good selection of interesting details and some effective use of language, but the piece is poorly organised (especially the second paragraph). Some details could be developed to be more interesting. Sentences tend to be simple, sometimes incorrectly punctuated, with some grammatical errors. However, the final paragraph is an improvement.

Text 2 Caving

Caving, or pot-holing, as it is often known, means exploring underground passages. These passages are formed naturally over thousands of years by streams eroding limestone rock. This occurs in several areas in Britain, especially in Yorkshire, Derbyshire, Somerset, Devon and South Wales. Many of these passages still have streams running through them, but in others the streams have sunk out of sight. Some form complex maze-like networks stretching for miles and descending a hundred metres or more below the surface.

To cave safely, you need to be properly equipped and to go with experienced cavers. In wet caves, you need a wetsuit or waterproof oversuit, though in drier caves you could wear old clothes with a boiler suit on top. Special equipment includes flexible steel ladders, lifelining ropes and karabiners for 'pitches' – vertical drops.

Cavers are attracted to their sport for several reasons. First, there is the sporting challenge involved in clambering and squeezing through passages. Some cave passages are also beautifully decorated with stalactites and stalagmites formed by calcite dripping out of the rock. Perhaps above all there is the sense of getting right away from the worries of the ordinary world.

Opening sentence explaining title

Explanation using technical terms

Good verb – better than 'going down'

Appropriate use of second person verb 'you'

Effective topic sentence

Accurate and interesting adjectives

Concise explanation of term using dash

Vivid verbs – better than 'getting'

Gives sense of conclusion

Overall comment on Text 2

An informative explanation, well-structured (what and where, what you need, why), with appropriate use and fluent explanation of specialist terms, and explanation of things that the reader might not know about. Concise expression, with occasionally interesting word choices.

Check your progress

Give your description marks out of 3 for how well the following writing techniques have been used.

⇨ topic sentences   [3] ....

⇨ helpful structure   [3] ....

⇨ ending with a sense of completion (not just stopping at random)   [3] ....

⇨ well-chosen details, effective word choices   [3] ...

⇨ appropriate selection and explanation of information   [3] ...

⇨ accurate spelling, punctuation, grammar with consistent tenses   [3] ...

Check your total out of 18

Overall, **how successful was your text?**

PARTIALLY 1 9 18 FULLY

Progress further

If you need to improve your writing, choose where to focus your effort. You could look again at pages 144–145. Then redraft your text. Where have you improved? If you need to, set further targets.

If your writing is high quality, congratulations! Now try this more challenging task using around 300 words:

Write an informative guide to the area where you live suitable for American families who will be based in the area for several months.

Assess your progress – writing summaries

When you have completed **writing summaries** using pages 146–147, use the guide below to track your progress.

Assess your summary against the examples

- Read the summaries and comments.
- Is your summary closer to the qualities of Summary 1, or Summary 2?

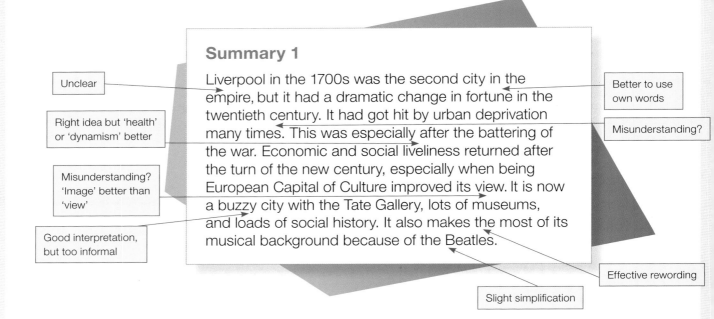

Summary 1

Unclear

Right idea but 'health' or 'dynamism' better

Misunderstanding? 'Image' better than 'view'

Good interpretation, but too informal

Liverpool in the 1700s was the second city in the empire, but it had a dramatic change in fortune in the twentieth century. It had got hit by urban deprivation many times. This was especially after the battering of the war. Economic and social liveliness returned after the turn of the new century, especially when being European Capital of Culture improved its view. It is now a buzzy city with the Tate Gallery, lots of museums, and loads of social history. It also makes the most of its musical background because of the Beatles.

Better to use own words

Misunderstanding?

Effective rewording

Slight simplification

Overall comment on Summary 1

A reasonable effort, though slightly too long. Some misunderstandings, and too much use of exact words from the source. Some effective paraphrasing and interpretation, though some word choices could be improved.

Summary 2

In the 1700s, Liverpool was the second most important British city, but it went into a serious decline in the twentieth century, especially after 1945. However, there were big economic and social improvements after 2000, especially when it became European Capital of Culture in 2008. It is now an energetic city with its own Tate Gallery, museums, and an interesting social history. It also capitalises on its great musical heritage, as befits the home town of the Beatles.

Fluent, concise subordinated sentence summing up points

Helpful signposting words

Effective paraphrase

Fluent rewording in subordinate clause

Overall comment on Summary 2

A fluent and concise summary. Effective paraphrasing and fluent use of concise, subordinated sentences. Clear understanding of original text. Good use of 'signposting' words.

Check your progress

Give your summary marks out of 3 for how well the following writing techniques have been used.

⇨ fluent use of own words where possible   [3] ....
⇨ use of appropriate signposting words and phrases   [3] ....
⇨ effective interpretation and paraphrasing of original   [3] ....
⇨ effective selection of important points   [3] ...
⇨ use of concise subordinated sentences   [3] ...
⇨ accurate spelling, punctuation and grammar   [3] ...

Check your total out of 18

Overall, **how successful was your summary?**

PARTIALLY | 1 | 9 | 18 | FULLY

Progress further

If you need to improve your writing, choose where to focus your effort. You could look again at pages 146–147. Then redraft your summary. Where have you improved? If you need to, set further targets.

If your writing is high quality, congratulations! Now try this more challenging task:

Summarise the whole article in 110–125 words.

Assess your progress – writing instruction texts

When you have completed **writing instruction texts** using pages 148–149, use this guide to track your progress.

Assess your instructions against the examples

- Read the sets of instructions and comments.
- Is your writing closer to the qualities of Text 1, or Text 2?

Text 1
Use the school lunch system

1: You need to put stuff on your tray in the canteen. The teacher will let you in to queue.

2: Take drink from drinks cabinet, hot dishes from servery and dessert from sweets counter.

4: Use finger scanner at pay station. Picture pops up.

5: Green light should flash. If red one then it hasn't worked.

6: Wait while dinner lady keys in your items.

7: Take tray to table with whoever your mates are and eat lunch.

8: When finished, tip and stack.

Should come first

Correct term but needs information (works on fingerprint)

Helpful indicator, but then what?

Say 'tip leftovers in food waste bin and stack plates and tray'

Unclear and too informal

Helpful tips

Unclear (it means a picture of pupil for identification)

Too informal and too wordy

Overall comment on Text 1

These instructions are in manageable steps and almost correct in sequence. However, the language is sometimes unclear, and missing some key information. Wording could be more concise and is sometimes too informal.

Text 2
Turn on computer, log in and find a webpage

1: Press circular green button on front of computer tower (not screen) to turn on.

2: Wait a few seconds for computer to boot up and for login box to appear.

3: Enter your user name, all lower case (assigned by IT, e.g. s.davies5), in first box.

4: Enter your password in second box (case-sensitive, at least 7 characters, including upper and lower case letters, and at least one number).

5: If your login details are correct, the school home page will appear when you click Enter.

6: Enter name of webpage required in navigation bar at top-left of webpage and click Enter, or enter "google.co.uk" and search for keywords, or whole phrase in double quotation marks.

7: Choose page from entries and click to open it, or right-click to open it in a new window so that you can easily return to the list.

Simple and precise imperative

Correct terms and sequence

Helpful details

Good use of subordinated sentence

Offers alternatives

Explains why this might be helpful

Overall comment on Text 2

A precise and helpful set of instructions with information presented concisely and in the correct order. Appropriate use of verbs, and an appropriately neutral register – not too formal or informal. Subordinated sentences improve flow of ideas.

Check your progress

Give your instructions marks out of 3 for how well the following writing techniques have been used.

⇨ Information broken into manageable steps [3] ....
⇨ Steps correctly sequenced [3] ....
⇨ Correct use of imperatives and other verb forms [3] ....
⇨ Use of one or more subordinated sentences [3] ...
⇨ Clear, precise, concise language [3] ...
⇨ Accurate spelling, punctuation and grammar [3] ...

Check your total out of 18

Overall, **how successful were your instructions?**

PARTIALLY 1 9 18 **FULLY**

Progress further

If you need to improve your writing, choose where to focus your effort. You could look again at pages 148–149. Then redraft your instructions. Where have you improved? If you need to, set further targets.

If your writing is high quality, congratulations! Now try this more challenging task using around 150 words:

Write a set of instructions for searching for an image online, copying it, and pasting it into a Word document.

Assess your progress – writing to persuade

When you have completed **writing to persuade** using pages 150–151, use this guide to track your progress.

Assess your appeal against the examples

- Read the appeals and comments.
- Is your writing closer to the qualities of Appeal 1, or Appeal 2?

Appeal 1 School uniform

School uniform is a waste of time. Why should everyone have to look the same? It's not as if the teachers have to wear it. The idea is it's fair because everyone has the same shirt, sweatshirt and tie so no one gets to come in wearing expensive new designer stuff every day. Some kids still have smarter and newer uniform than others. It's also so we can be identified if we're doing bad things like shoplifting sweets. That makes us feel like prisoners who have to wear stripy uniform so they can be spotted if they escape!

We should be allowed to wear our own clothes and express ourselves. We don't want to look like sausages all in a row. Anyway, it's still not fair because school uniform suits some people better than others. I mean, maroon is not my colour! What's more, it's not a good preparation for life because you don't have to wear uniform in most jobs.

So, basically, sign this petition and we can start wearing what we want!

Annotations:
- Effective rhetorical question
- Too informal
- Topic sentence, but language could be more interesting
- Good argument, but should be in paragraph 1
- States case but without any interesting language
- Anticipates counter-argument
- Good argument, but should be linked to previous sentence
- Quite a good simile
- Call to action, but simplistic

Overall comment on Appeal 1

Some good arguments, with some quite effective rhetorical techniques, such as the use of rhetorical question and simile. More signposting would make the appeal more fluent. Some more interesting or emotive language would also help to improve this.

Appeal 2 High Speed rail

The London–Scotland High Speed rail link will, if it is ever allowed to go ahead, create massive disruption. Thousands of families will be forced to sell up and move elsewhere. Tenants whose rented homes get in the way of this monster of modern planning gone mad will be out on the street. This outrage will happen across a huge swathe of London, from Euston northwards, and again as the line enters Birmingham. In between, countless communities will be smashed or split apart by the line itself and by the noise of trains travelling at 250mph. Yet most will be too far from a station to use the service themselves.

In between cities, the line will slash through the green belt around London, gouging its way through the precious landscape and unique natural habitats of the Chilterns, disrupting scenery and wildlife wherever it goes.

Work is due to begin in 2017, so there is still time to stop this madness. The government should be focusing on helping more people to work from home, or get to work on local transport, not funding a £60 billion project to benefit fat cat business travellers. Please help to keep Britain green and save it from High Speed rail. Sign our petition now.

Sub-clause emphasises still just a proposal

Strong verb

Emotive personification

Emotive verbs

Positive emotive language

Presents alternative

Emotive language; alliteration

Positive 'call to action'

Overall comment on Appeal 2

A well-structured persuasive appeal, using a mixture of factual detail and emotive language to contrast negative and positive outcomes. Effective use of rhetorical techniques – personification and alliteration.

• •

Check your progress

Give your appeal marks out of 3 for how well the following writing techniques have been used.

⇨ logical structure [3] ....
⇨ use of some facts and details [3] ....
⇨ emotive language [3] ....
⇨ variety of sentence types [3] ...
⇨ use of language techniques such as alliteration [3] ...
⇨ accurate spelling, punctuation, grammar with consistent past/present [3] ...

Check your total out of 18

Overall, **how successful was the writing in your appeal?**

PARTIALLY 1 9 18 FULLY

Progress further

If you need to improve your writing, choose where to focus your effort. You could look again at pages 150–151. Then redraft your appeal. Where have you improved? If you need to, set further targets.

If your writing is high quality, congratulations! Now try this more challenging task using around 300 words:

Write a persuasive speech arguing that TV adverts aimed at children should be banned.

Assess your progress – writing an expository or narrative essay

When you have completed **writing an expository or narrative essay** using pages 152–153, use this guide to track your progress.

Assess your essay against the examples

- Read the essays and comments.
- Is your writing closer to the qualities of Essay 1, or Essay 2?

Essay 1

We were 2–1 down in our final match of the season, with five minutes to go before the final whistle. I had been picked for the team as a last-minute decision because Gareth Jones had a dodgy knee. It was the idea of the teacher in charge, Mr Costa. I think he wanted to see what I could do, and maybe boost my confidence a bit after what had happened.

The Smallfield winger fouled our captain, Darren, it seemed like our big chance. It was a free kick in the penalty area. Darren was still limping and pulling a face, but I was literally gobsmacked when he said, 'Right, Carver, you take the kick.' I thought maybe he wanted to show the teacher it was the wrong choice to put me in and I was rubbish. He's like that. I don't know why he's captain. Probably because his mum's a dinner lady or something.

I put the ball in position. I stepped back a few paces. I looked hard at one end of the goal. Then I ran and changed position at the last moment. The other side didn't know I'm left-footed. The ball went right over their heads and landed in the back of the net. The goalie did a dive but the wrong way. Suddenly I was man of the match.

Annotations:
- More information than we need
- Intriguing mystery – never solved!
- Inaccurate cliché
- Better as a single sentence
- Gives context
- Comma splice
- Keep to the point
- Slight mis-sequencing; too suddenly wrapped up

Overall comment on Essay 1

Good account, with some helpful context, but too much background getting in the way. Some good sentences, but would be improved by more subordinated sentences and some more original and interesting word choices. Conclusion could be more effective, perhaps linked to the unsolved mystery in paragraph 1.

Essay 2

My family always rents a canal boat in the summer. It is an almost dreamlike way to travel – most of the time. One year we were cruising the Worcester and Birmingham Canal, which runs through peaceful pastures with grazing cows. Unfortunately it also has a lot of locks – devices which get a boat up or downhill by turning the canal into a kind of staircase. At every lock we had to sail in, close the gates, open the 'paddles' to let out the water so that the boat dropped down, then open the lower gates and sail on.

By the time we reached Tardebigge – thirty narrow locks one after the other, Dad had a bad back, so I was helping with the locks. In the third lock, Dad loosely tied the boat to a bollard, and went to look at the next lock. As the water swirled away, I realised with horror that the rope had tightened on the bollard and the boat was being hoisted up on its side like a dog on a tight lead. My mum and baby sister were inside, and in seconds the boat would keel over.

With no time to think, I rushed to the front gates, and managed to wind down the paddles to stop the water level dropping. Then I ran and opened the top paddles to let in water to raise the boat. It was nearly a disaster, but I'd learned that I could rely on myself to act fast in an emergency!

Annotations:
- Effective account, with hint at what is to come
- Signposting word
- Interesting verb
- Sense of drama
- Sets scene, preparing for contrast
- Succinct explanation
- Effective simile
- Suspense
- Sequencing word

Overall comment on Essay 2

An effective account, setting the scene, creating atmosphere, and hinting at drama to come. Just enough explanation is given. Some interesting and effective word choices and techniques. Good use of signposting words. Appropriate conclusion.

Check your progress

Give your description marks out of 3 for how well the following writing techniques have been used.

⇨ setting scene or context   [3] ....
⇨ revealing information in an effective order   [3] ....
⇨ helping the flow of the writing by using signposting (linking) words   [3] ....
⇨ well chosen details, effective word choices, appeal to senses   [3] ...
⇨ use of language techniques such as imagery   [3] ...
⇨ accurate spelling, punctuation and grammar with consistent tenses   [3] ...

Check your total out of 18

Overall, **how successful was your essay?**

PARTIALLY   1   9   18   FULLY

Progress further

If you need to improve your writing, choose where to focus your effort. You could look again at pages 152–153. Then redraft your essay. Where have you improved? If you need to, set further targets.

If your writing is high quality, congratulations! Now try this more challenging task using around 350 words:

Write an essay explaining what you think will be the main challenges to people of your age in a changing world as they grow older.

6 Assess your progress – writing to describe

When you have completed **writing to describe** using pages 154–155, use this guide to track your progress.

> **Assess your description against the examples**
> - Read the descriptions and comments.
> - Is your writing closer to the qualities of Description 1, or Description 2?

Introduces the place and what the writer feels about it, but it needs to say why it's great

Description 1

The park near where I live is a great place to visit. In summer people sit on the rows of benches by the bandstand and eat their lunch. Sometimes they throw crumbs to the pigeons and sparrows that flock nearby hoping for a meal. Down by the boating lake there are droopy willow trees that hang down like hair. Big brown and black geese sit around beneath them, or cruise around on the lake.

In summer you can hire rowing boats on the lake, and you can hear the shrieks of girls getting splashed or thinking they are going to capsize. You can also see big carp coming up to the surface.

You can also usually see some skateboarders showing off or kids on BMX bikes doing wheelies. Then there's a playground but the best rides have been taken out for health and safety. All in all there's a lot going on.

Good detail, but the description could be more interesting. What sort of people?

Good detail and verb choice

Appealing detail but dull description. Other words for 'big' and 'coming'?

Good details, adjective and vivid simile

Lively description with sense appeal; could develop it (e.g. 'piercing shrieks')

Lively details; could be expanded

Writer attempts a conclusion but it is rather dull

Overall comment on Description 1

Some good choices of details and effective use of language (e.g. the trees), but some of the language is rather dull (e.g. 'a great place', 'people sit on the rows'). Some details could be developed to be more interesting (e.g. 'a lunchtime paradise', 'schoolkids, OAPs and pin-striped business types sit ...')

Description 2

Bargain Wood is a wild and secluded place where, most days, you won't meet another soul. A rocky stream leaps, rushes and cascades three hundred feet down from Cleddon Falls, and even in summer it is cold enough to numb your hand in seconds. In winter its waterfalls are clustered with icicles. Deer pick their way cautiously down through the beech trees to drink here at night, leaving only their hoof-prints in the mud to show where they have walked. By day they vanish into the trees and undergrowth like mist in the morning sun.

The ground is steep, but a zigzag path climbs up like a switchback through the trees. Here and there the walker has to ford a little stream or climb over a fallen tree. At first, the wood seems empty and quiet, except for the gurgling of water and the whispering of the wind in the treetops. But if you stop and listen, you might hear the song of a robin, or the chattering call of a blackbird.

Most mysterious, here and there, in rocky hollows, almost hidden by leaves in summer, are the remains of ancient homes. Mossy, rough-cut walls remain, all that survives of those who once lived in these woods.

Annotations:
- Opening sentence sums up place, using two good adjectives
- Triplet of lively verbs
- Sense appeal
- Good adverb
- Appealing, atmospheric details and appropriate simile
- Good simile
- Well-chosen details with sense appeal
- Description comes to a tantalising climax

Overall comment on Description 2

A description that creates an impression of this being a magical place. Well-chosen details (e.g. the icicles), sense appeal (e.g. 'cold enough to numb your hand'), effective word choices (e.g. 'cascades') and use of language techniques.

Check your progress

Give your description marks out of 3 for how well the following writing techniques have been used.

⇨ opening sentence that makes the reader want to read on [3] ....
⇨ developing and linking / contrasting ideas [3] ....
⇨ ending with a sense of completion (not just stopping at random) [3] ....
⇨ well-chosen details, effective word choices, appeal to senses [3] ...
⇨ use of language techniques such as imagery, repetition [3] ...
⇨ accurate spelling, punctuation, grammar with consistent past/present [3] ...

Check your total out of 18

Overall, **how successful was your description?**

PARTIALLY — 1 — 9 — 18 — FULLY

Progress further

If you need to improve your writing, choose where to focus your effort. You could look again at pages 154–155. Then redraft your description. Where have you improved? If you need to, set further targets.

If your writing is high quality, congratulations! Now try this more challenging task using around 400 words:

Write a description of a place that shows signs of the distant past: a churchyard with old gravestones, a ruined castle, or a crumbling old house.

Assess your progress – writing the opening of a story

When you have completed **the opening paragraphs of your story of a challenge** using pages 156–157, use the guide below to track your progress in writing to describe.

> **Assess your description against the example paragraphs**
> - Read the comments about the quality of the writing.
> - For each of the different areas, is the quality of your writing closer to Opening paragraphs 1, or Opening paragraphs 2?

Opening uses realistic conversation to interest readers, making them wonder what the argument is about.

Opening paragraphs 1

The first line introduces the two characters who face the challenge.

'Well, the big day! And look who it is!' said Grace as she came over to Janera. 'Think you can play with the big people now? Have you ever jumped a proper fence and not just little training jumps?'

The character's sneering comments introduce the gymkhana and show she does not think Janera is a good rider.

'We'll see when it comes to it, won't we?' Janera replied.

The idea of Janera thinking she might be good enough to win develops the challenge.

It was the day of the race when Janera first thought she might win. She knew that it was a long shot but all her training must have helped. When she'd seen her rival, Grace, across the field earlier in the day, she thought she could see a bit of weakness in the way she was looking at the fences. Her horse was called Ludo. He looked good but her horse Myoko was better. He could jump fences well. She'd been training and he had got better and better she thought.

Janera's reply shows she will stand up for herself. However, the conversation could be developed to strengthen the opening.

Could emphasise the description of Janera's training better.

This description of 'weakness' could be strengthened.

The horses could be described more fully to strengthen the contest between them.

The phrase 'better and better' could be made more effective by describing her improvements.

Overall comment on Opening paragraphs 1

An effective opening that introduces the challenge between the two characters. The conversation shows their feelings but could have been lengthened. The idea of the 'weakness' is important and needed to be more effectively described. More powerful description (the horses and the training) would have strengthened the opening.

Opening paragraphs 2

After the storm ended, the track lay glistening brightly in the sudden sunshine. The crowd streamed from the entrance towards the grandstands clutching their prized tickets like gold coins. Rising above the excited chatter of children swarming around their parents was the tantalising roar of highly-tuned engines and the frantic screech of the sound system as the commentators attempted to describe the scene.

The bright gleam of laptop screens drew all eyes to the gloom of the pits where the engineers quietly punched in numbers setting up each car for the race. Nervously, the mechanics hovered behind the engineers awaiting their instructions for all the final adjustments to the complex machines. At the heart of each team's pit area, lay the gorgeously painted cars wrapped and cosseted like valuable jewels awaiting their chance to shine in front of every eye.

Finally, the crowd's buzz was stilled as the drivers emerged from the back of each pit in their elaborate suits covered in logos like armoured knights wearing their favours at a medieval joust . At the head of the line was the familiar figure of Giorgio Luis in the gold and red while beside him, all in black, strode Ashley Prince. The two exchanged the merest glance but everyone who saw it knew it meant that this was going to be the race of the season.

Annotations:
- Use of sound to build excitement
- Simile of the jewels used effectively to describe the racing cars
- Opening description gives a clear impression of the setting
- Simile suggests how valuable the tickets are for the crowd
- Good use of contrast in moving to describe the darker pits and the quiet engineers
- Good use of contrast with the noise of the first paragraph to build excitement
- Well-chosen simile used to describe the appearance of the drivers
- Powerful use of a small detail to focus on the challenge between the two drivers

Overall comment on Opening paragraphs 2

Powerful description used to create the setting and build the sense of excitement. Good use of sound description (sound of the crowd, engines, hush as the drivers emerge) creates anticipation. Strong similes (drivers like knights, cars like jewels) add to the description. Accurate choice of verbs to convey atmosphere (mechanics hovered, cars wrapped and cosseted) in the scene. Powerful use of tiny detail at the end (merest glance) to set up the challenge.

Check your progress

Give your opening paragraphs marks out of 3 for how well the following writing techniques have been used.

⇨ opening that draws the reader in making them want to read on　　　[3] ....
⇨ powerful description of the setting　　　[3] ....
⇨ building up the challenge between the characters　　　[3] ....
⇨ well-chosen details, effective word choices, appeal to senses　　　[3] ...
⇨ use of language techniques such as imagery, repetition　　　[3] ...
⇨ accurate spelling, punctuation, grammar with consistent past/present tense　　　[3] ...

Check your total out of 18

Overall, **how successful was your description?**

PARTIALLY　1　9　18　FULLY

Progress further

If you need to improve your writing, look again at what most needs to improve. You could look again at pages 156–157. Then redraft the opening to your story. Where have you improved? If you need to, set further targets for improvement.

If your writing is high quality, congratulations! Now try this more challenging task using around 400 words:
Complete your story developing the challenge between the two characters you have introduced. Remember to bring your story to an effective conclusion that satisfies your readers.

Assess your progress – writing a recount

When you have completed **recounts** using pages 158–159, use the guide below to track your progress.

Assess your recount against the examples

- Read the comments about the quality of the writing.
- For each of the different areas, is the quality of your writing closest to Recount 1, or Recount 2?

The correct information begins the recount but important details are missing: which young people, which mountain was climbed, when was the climb, how did they climb on bikes?

The events in the recount are not written in a logical order.

Including a quote from the headteacher is a good feature but the name of the head and the school should have been provided.

The fact that they also paddled canoes should have been mentioned in the beginning.

Recount 1

Mountain climb success
Some young people climbed a mountain recently on bicycles. It was a real challenge for them and they were really tired at the end of the climb. They travelled there in a school mini-bus driven by a teacher. They decided to climb the mountain for charity and they asked the whole school to choose the charity.

Their headteacher said: 'We are really proud at the school that they decided to take on this challenge. When young people are criticised so much it is good to know that they want to help people less fortunate than themselves.'

As well as the mountain they climbed in Wales, they also paddled canoes over a large lake. They took about a day to do the climb. Scott Chaim, one of the pupils said: 'It was one of the hardest things we have ever done but we are all pleased it was a success.'

Clear headline to attract readers, but could have been made more exciting with words like 'challenging' or 'gruelling' to emphasise the difficulty.

Describing the selection of the charity is positive but the charity should have been named.

A very good quote to have been included.

Ends with a strong quote and the name of the young person is included.

Overall comment on Recount 1

A good headline is used for the recount though it could have been more powerful and exciting. There are good features such as the use of quotes from the headteacher and a student. The recount lacks the basic details such as where the climb took place, how they climbed, when it happened and who was involved. The order of the recount needed to be more logical without the introduction of new information later on that this recount shows.

Good headline with powerful language and alliteration to make it memorable

Opening sentence contains the key information (where, when, who)

The second paragraph gives more detail about the singer and how she became famous

Recount 2

Superstar sensation for shoppers

Excited shoppers got more than they bargained for at the Tudorgrange Shopping Centre in Taylorford last Friday 31st May when singing superstar Tania gave an unexpected performance at Laidlaw's department store. The show was organised to celebrate 60 years since Laidlaw's first opened in Taylorford.

The second sentence explains why the event was taking place (60 years since the shop opened)

The songs she sang are given and it is explained that she had to leave the performance for a TV recording

Tania, 23, is the sensational winner of last year's Upcoming Stars TV talent show. Her first single the fabulous ballad Blooms was a huge success breaking records for downloads in the first 48 hours. At Friday's show she included Blooms and several other numbers she covered during last year's competition. The free show lasted for 35 minutes before the superstar was whisked away by security staff for a TV recording in Edinburgh.

Delighted shopper Chris Crooms, 39, said: 'It's not every day that you see someone so famous when you are out for a coffee and window-shopping.' Her daughter Charlotte 16 agreed: 'I managed to get Tania's autograph before she left. I will never forget this day, the best shopping trip I've ever been on.' Laidlaw's manager Tim McKenzie, 47, said: 'It was a great success and we hoped the shoppers enjoyed it as much as we did. I wonder who will be performing at Laidlaw's when it is 120 years old.'

Quotes from shoppers who saw the show give clear personal reactions

Quote from the shop manager sums up the success of the event

Final part of the quote links back to the reason for the show and forward to the future

Overall comment on Recount 2

A clear and entertaining recount with an engaging headline to interest and intrigue readers. The key details are all included: where, when, who, what and how. Further details are included to give more background information about the singer and how she became famous through a talent contest. Appropriate quotes with details of who is speaking made clear.

Check your progress

Give your description marks out of 3 for how well the following writing techniques have been used.

⇨ headline that makes the reader want to read the story   [3] ....
⇨ the key details (where, when, who, why how) are included at the start   [3] ....
⇨ further information given to expand the key details   [3] ....
⇨ precise descriptions with effective language chosen   [3] ...
⇨ comments from people who were involved   [3] ...
⇨ accurate spelling, punctuation, grammar with consistent use of past tense   [3] ...

Check your total out of 18

Overall, **how successful was your description?**

PARTIALLY | 1 | 9 | 18 | FULLY

Progress further

If you need to improve your writing, look again at what most needs to improve. You could look again at pages 158–159. Then redraft your recount. Where have you improved? If you need to, set further targets for improvement.

If your writing is high quality, congratulations! Now try this more challenging task using around 400 words:

Extend your own recount to include more details about what happened and quotes from some of the people who were involved.

Glossary

Active voice: Writing in the active voice means constructing sentences where the subject 'acts', e.g. 'I ate the sandwich'. Sentences in the active voice are direct and it is clear who is doing what.

Adjective: A 'describing' word, the main role of which is to give more information about a noun e.g. 'the red balloon'; 'the unhappy child'.

> **Adjectival phrase**: An adjectival phrase adds detail to a noun, e.g. *'Dressed in a smart suit,* Dermot stood up to speak.'

> **Adjectival clause**: An adjectival clause adds detail to a noun, e.g. 'Dermot, *who is always immaculate,* introduced the first contestant;' 'I am worried about the weather, *which looks threatening.'*

Adverb: A word that adds detail to a verb or adjective, e.g. *quickly, slowly, hesitantly, rapidly, completely.*

> **Adverbial clause**: A clause that does the same work as an adverb: it adds detail to the verb, e.g. *'Because Lucy couldn't swim,* she sat by the pool.'

> **Adverbial phrase**: A short phrase that adds detail to a verb, e.g. 'Lucy swam *very slowly.'*

Agreement: This usually refers to grammatical agreement between a verb and its subject, e.g. 'The *girls run* quickly'; 'the *girl ran yesterday'.* The main forms of agreement are between person, e.g. 'I *am'* vs 'he *is';* 'we *were'* vs 'he *was';* and number, e.g. 'the boy *runs'* (singular) vs 'the boys *run'* (plural).

Alliteration: The use of repeated consonant sounds usually at the beginnings of words.

Annotate: To make brief notes on a text in order to highlight certain features.

Argument: In argumentative writing, the writer chooses which facts to present in order to present a case or argue for one point of view.

Assonance: The repetition of vowel sounds within phrases or sentences, e.g. 'And the moon rose over an open field.'

Atmosphere: The mood, emotion or feeling that is conveyed by the setting in a story. A writer creates the sense of a particular place so that the reader can almost experience it for themselves.

Autobiography: A life story written in the first person.

Biography: A life story written in the third person, by someone who has access to a person's life.

Clause: A group of words that express a complete idea, usually consisting of a *subject*, *verb* and *object*.

> **Conditional clause**: Conditional subordinate clauses begin with *if* or *unless*, e.g. *'Unless you leave now*, I will call the police.'

> **Main clause**: A main clause is a clause that can stand by itself (also known as a single-clause sentence). A main clause contains a subject and a predicate; it makes sense by itself.

> **Subordinate clause**: A clause that cannot stand on its own as a sentence.

Cliché: This is an image that has become stale through overuse.

Conjunction: Words that link words or clauses within a sentence (e.g. and, but, or).

Connective: Words or phrases that link clauses or sentences (e.g. because, therefore, on the other hand).

Draft: Any of the stages in the development of a piece of writing before it becomes final.

Edit: To alter and revise a piece of writing in order to improve it.

Emotive language: Emotive language aims to get an emotional response. It can be serious, as in charity appeals, or it can use a lighter approach to express a viewpoint.

Essay: A piece of writing which is usually written from the author's personal point of view, and expresses their own ideas about a topic.

> **Expository essay**: In an expository essay, you 'expose' your ideas and feelings and explain them interestingly.

> **Narrative essay**: A narrative essay tells a true story, e.g. an account of an experience.

Explanation: A text which explains usually presents some facts, but unlike a simple information text, it shows how they relate to each other. It is likely to do one of two things:

- enable the reader to understand an idea or concept;
- present a process, showing a sequence of cause and effect.

Formality: In writing, this is the use of serious vocabulary, expressions and standard grammar. Formal writing tends to make more use of subordinated sentences, and uses more polite vocabulary, avoiding colloquial expressions.

Fronted adverbial: An adverb, adverbial phrase or clause that starts a sentence, e.g. 'Creaking eerily, the shed door began to open.'

Informality: Informal writing is closer to spoken language. It may include more colloquial expressions such as slang, figures of speech and asides. Informal writing takes a personal tone as if you were speaking directly to your audience (the reader).

Information texts: Information texts present facts and ideas in a clear and logical way. They are usually written in the present tense.

Instructions: An instructional text uses precise language, breaks information up into well-ordered steps, and uses imperative verbs. Instructional texts often combine words and pictures.

Internal rhyme: Rhyming words occurring in the middle of a line rather than just at the end, e.g. 'As if a rose should close and be a bud again.'

Metaphor: A word picture that brings something to life by describing it as if it is something else that is similar in at least one way, but different in others, e.g. 'You are *a brick wall over which I must climb* in order to succeed.'

Narrative voice: Who is telling the story. This can be the writer, or a character in the story. (*see* **Point of view**).

First person: A story told by one of the characters using 'I', 'me', 'my'. This can make the story seem very vivid and immediate. As the narrator tells the story, they can express something of their own character.

Third person: A story told by the writer, who can express what characters think and feel.

Noun: A noun is a word used to name a person, animal, place, thing, an abstract idea.

Noun clause: A noun clause is one which does the job of a noun in a sentence. It can be the *subject* or the *object*, e.g. 'What I do for a living usually disgusts people.' (Subject) 'Everyone thinks that you're very brave.' (Object)

Noun phrase: Two or more words (a phrase) that do the job of a noun in a sentence, e.g. 'This sentence contains two noun phrases.'

Object: A word or group of words in a sentence that is acted on by the subject, e.g. 'Joe ran past the shops'; 'She called him on her mobile.'

Onomatopoeia: The use of words that echo the sound they describe, e.g. 'buzz'; 'fizz'; 'crash'.

Paragraph: A self-contained, coherent 'chunk' of meaning made up of several sentences dealing with a particular point, topic or idea.

Passive voice: Sentences where the subject is 'passive' – it is acted upon, rather than being an agent of action, e.g. 'Petrol prices were increased this year by 10 per cent.' Use the passive in more formal writing, or if you want to 'hide' the 'agent' (who was doing it).

Personification: Describes an abstract thing or idea as if it were a living thing, e.g. 'The wolves of hunger howl outside the poor man's door.'

Perspective: In writing, 'perspective' is the *view* or *outlook* of a text or a writer on a particular issue or topic (*see* **Point of view**).

Persuasion: A persuasive text seeks to make the reader do or believe something. It employs a range of techniques to argue a particular point of view, or to make the reader want to act: these are often called 'persuasive devices'.

Point of view: A text can be written from one 'point of view' – in other words, showing what happens from one perspective, which could be a character, or a narrator, or the writer (*see* **Narrative voice** and **Perspective**).

Predicate: The part of the clause that states something about the subject. Typically it is made up of a verb and what follows the verb.

Prefix: A group of letters placed at the start of a word (the 'stem' word) that alter either its meaning or how the word is used. Examples of common prefixes include: '*un*' and '*im*' meaning 'not' as in '*un*happy' or '*im*polite'; '*re*' meaning 'again' as in '*re*do', or '*re*view'.

Pronoun: A pronoun is a word that is used in place of a noun. Pronouns come in many shapes and sizes: *personal* pronouns such as 'I'; 'me'; 'we'; *demonstrative* pronouns such as 'this' 'that', 'these' and 'those'; *relative* pronouns such as 'who', 'which' 'what'; *interrogative* pronouns such as 'why', and 'who' which are used to ask questions; and *indefinite* pronouns such as 'one', 'someone', 'nobody', 'everything'.

Use pronouns to make your sentences less repetitive as you don't have to keep repeating the same noun.

Proofread: Read through a final version of a text very carefully to pick out any errors that need correcting.

Quotation: A short extract, inside inverted commas, that is used as evidence when you are analysing a text.

Recount: A non-fiction text that tells the facts or the true story of something. Usually told using the past tense, and in chronological (time) sequence. Many newspaper reports are 'recounts'.

Register: The type of language used in a particular social setting or writing context; e.g. a formal or informal register, or a scientific register.

Resolution: In literature, this is the point in the story where a conflict or a plot line reaches its conclusion.

Rhetoric: The art and study of how to write and speak effectively and convincingly.

Rhetorical effect: Writers use a range of rhetorical *techniques*, such as repetition, making a point with three words or phrases, or using lists, to drive home an argument or to convey their meaning with impact.

Rhyme: Repetition of similar sounds in two or more words, usually at the ends of lines in poems and songs.

Rhythm: A musical quality in writing made up of a series of repeated beats in words.

Sentence: One or more words that make sense on their own, and are linked together by their grammar. Most sentences contain a *finite verb*.

> **Single-clause sentence**: Single-clause sentences contain one main clause, usually made up of a subject, verb and object.

> **Multi-clause sentence**: Contains two or more clauses linked by co-ordination or subordination.

>> **Co-ordination**: Sentences with more than one main clause, usually joined by a co-ordinating conjuction: *and, but, or*.

>> **Cumulative sentence**: A long sentence based on an independent clause, to which detail is added by several subordinate clauses or phrases, so that meaning accumulates.

Subordination: Sentences including a *main clause* (a phrase which makes complete sense on its own) and one or more *subordinate clauses* (Which depend on the main clause to make sense).

Simile: A simile is a kind of word picture using 'like', 'as' or 'than', also known as a figure of speech. It brings something to life by comparing it with something that is similar in at least one important way, but different in others, e.g.
'A rugby player since childhood, Davies had *legs like oak trees*.'

Style: Style in writing refers to the overall way that a text is written, e.g. how a story is told, or an argument presented. It includes all the key features of the writing such as point of view, word choice, grammar, use of imagery.

Subject: The name for the word or words which occurs with (and often before) a verb. The subject of a sentence is usually a noun or a noun phrase.

Summary: A shortened version of a text containing the most important information.

Synthesis: This is when you pull together different ideas into a single explanation or account.

Tense: In grammar, *tense* is how you indicate whether something is happening now (*present* tense); before now (*past* tense); or after now (*future* tense). *Verbs* often change in order to signal which tense they are in. They might change their form (as in 'I want*ed* to go there'), or use an auxiliary verb (as in 'I *will* want to go there'.)

Tension: Meaning literally 'stress from pulling something tight'; in literature it refers to the way a story can build up gradually to a climax, so that the reader 'feels' tense as they read.

Tone: The emotional quality of a piece of writing; e.g. angry, comic, sympathetic.

Verb: A class of words that express: an *action* (as in 'I run'); *state* (as in 'I feel …'); or *occurrence* (as in 'I became …').